The Matrimonial Homes (Family Protection) (Scotland) Act 1981

The Matrimonial Homes (Family Protection) (Scotland) Act 1981

SECOND EDITION

By

D. I. NICHOLS, M.A., Ph.D., W.S.

Sometime Major Scholar of Jesus College, Cambridge

and

M. C. MESTON, M.A., LL.B., J.D.

Professor of Private Law at Aberdeen University

EDINBURGH
W. GREEN & SON LTD.
St. Giles Street
1986

First published 1982
Second edition 1986

W. Green & Son Ltd.
ISBN 0 414 00778 6

PRINTED IN GREAT BRITAIN BY
Thomson Litho Limited
EAST KILBRIDE, SCOTLAND

PHOTOTYPESET BY
Waverley Graphics Limited
EDINBURGH, SCOTLAND

PREFACE TO SECOND EDITION

SINCE the first edition was published there have been many changes in the law relating to matrimonial homes. On the legislative front, the principal amendments are those made by the Law Reform (Miscellaneous Provisions) (Scotland) Act 1985, although the Family Law (Scotland) Act 1985 and the Bankruptcy (Scotland) Act 1985 have also had an effect. As expected there have been a considerable number of cases on exclusion orders, but, somewhat surprisingly, there is a dearth of reported authority on most other aspects of the Act.

The text has been considerably expanded to deal not only with the above changes, but also with the queries and difficulties that have arisen in practice. We are grateful to the many people who have brought problems to our attention and hope this feedback will continue. Revised styles of affidavits are included to take account of the new statutory formulae for protecting purchasers and creditors.

The opinions expressed are those of the authors alone and should not be taken to represent the views of any government department or body.

The law is stated as at 31 March 1986, but the text has been written as if the Family Law (Scotland) Act 1985 was in force.

D. I. NICHOLS.

M. C. MESTON.

April 1986.

PREFACE TO FIRST EDITION

THE purpose of this book is to state and explain the substantial changes in Scots law made by the Matrimonial Homes (Family Protection) (Scotland) Act 1981. The main effects of the Act are in the law relating to the matrimonial home and the enforcement of matrimonial interdicts. Many of the provisions, however, extend also to unmarried cohabiting couples.

It is hoped that this book will provide a guide through the provisions of the Act which will be of assistance to family law practitioners, conveyancers and students. The Act has effected so many changes that some may not have received the detailed attention they merit. The authors would be glad to receive suggestions for improvements.

The opinions expressed are those of the authors alone and should not be taken to represent the views of any government department.

The authors are grateful to the Law Society of Scotland for permission to reproduce their recommended styles for renunciations and affidavits which are contained in Appendix III.

Mr. D. J. McNeil, W.S., Mr. J. D. Robertson, and Mr. J. F. Wallace, Advocate, kindly read the manuscript and suggested many valuable amendments which are gratefully acknowledged.

Although the Act has not yet come into force, the text has been written as if this had already happened.

March 1982.

D. I. NICHOLS.
M. C. MESTON.

TABLE OF CONTENTS

TABLE OF CASES

[All references are to paragraph numbers]

Table of Cases

CHAPTER 1

INTRODUCTION

1–01. THE Matrimonial Homes (Family Protection) (Scotland) Act 1981 has two principal themes. These are the conferment of a right of occupation of the matrimonial home upon a spouse otherwise not entitled to occupancy, and the provision of more effective civil remedies against domestic violence. These apparently separate themes are closely related. A law which permits a husband to eject his wife from the matrimonial home at will encourages domestic violence since it reinforces the view, often held by violent men, that a wife should be subservient to her husband. The absence of a right to occupy the matrimonial home and the lack of any judicial power to exclude a violent proprietor presents the victim of domestic violence with a stark choice; either to endure violence as the price of remaining in the family home or to leave with the children for alternative accommodation which is often cramped and unsuitable.

1–02. It took a long time to achieve reform in this area. The Royal Commission on Marriage and Divorce which reported in 1956[1] made many recommendations regarding rights of occupation of the matrimonial home. These recommendations were implemented, albeit with substantial changes, for England and Wales by the Matrimonial Homes Act 1967. No similar legislation was enacted for Scotland. In the early 1970s a Select Committee of the House of Commons investigated violence in the family. Many of their recommendations were implemented by the Domestic Violence and Matrimonial Proceedings Act 1976 which again only extended to England and Wales. In response to the Select Committee's report[2] the Labour Government requested the Scottish Law Commission to consider and report on possible changes in the law to give additional protection to a spouse threatened with violence by the other spouse and whether a statutory right of occupation in the matrimonial home should be introduced in Scotland. In pursuance of that request the Scottish Law Commission issued a consultative memorandum in 1978.[3] After considering the many comments made by those consulted the Commission published a report[4] containing recommendations for reform of the law in those areas.

1–03. The Scottish Law Commission's recommendations were generally adopted by the Conservative Government and formed the basis of the Matrimonial Homes (Family Protection) (Scotland) Act 1981 ("the Act"). Substantial changes were made, however, in the protection afforded to

---

[1] Report of the Royal Commission on Marriage and Divorce, Cmd. 9678 (1956) (Morton Report).
[2] Report from the Select Committee on Violence in Marriage (1974-75; H.C. 553).
[3] Memorandum No. 41, *Family law: Occupancy Rights in the Matrimonial Home and Domestic Violence.*
[4] *Occupancy Rights in the Matrimonial Home and Domestic Violence,* Scot. Law Com. No. 60 (1980).

statutory occupancy rights against sales and other transactions relating to the matrimonial home which involve third parties. The important reforms contained in the Act brought Scots law into line with most other Commonwealth and Western European countries.

1–04. The Act consists of 23 sections. Sections 1 to 5 confer a right to occupy the matrimonial home together with subsidiary rights on the wife or husband of an entitled spouse (usually a sole owner or tenant). They also contain provisions enabling the courts to resolve disputes between couples which may arise now that either spouse is equally entitled to occupy the home. Sections 6 to 12 deal with the problem of protecting the statutory and other rights conferred by the Act against dealings between the entitled spouse and third parties or collusive diligence which would prejudice or defeat these rights. Section 13 empowers the court to transfer the tenancy of a matrimonial home from the tenant to his or her spouse, either during marriage or on divorce. Sections 14 to 17 enable the court to attach a power of arrest to certain civil interdicts and lay down the procedure following on an arrest for breach of such an interdict. Section 18 extends most of the provisions of the Act (but not ss. 6 to 12 and 19 to 21) to cohabiting couples. The remaining sections deal with minor and miscellaneous matters, and the interpretation and extent of the Act.

1–05. The Act came into force on 1 September 1982.[5] Like many other pieces of legislation it has not lived up to the expectations of those who campaigned for it. The first cases on exclusion orders were regarded as adopting a restrictive interpretation, although recent cases have taken a more liberal approach.[6] On the other hand, the complications introduced into residential conveyancing by the need to take account of the existence or possible existence of a non-entitled spouse's occupancy rights, while not as dire as prophesied by the Act's detractors, are nevertheless substantial.

1–06. Some of the problems that have emerged in the first three years have been dealt with by amending legislation,[7] but difficulties remain in the field of residential conveyancing and may yet need to be tackled. The amendments have been mainly concerned with clarifying the point in time in a sale or the taking of a security at which certain documents have to be delivered in order to avoid the non-entitled spouse's occupancy rights prevailing against the purchaser or lender.[8] Other useful changes include the clarification that a home provided for the purpose of living apart is not a matrimonial home,[9] extinction of statutory occupancy rights in the event of their non-exercise for five years after a sale of the home,[10] and entitling a non-entitled spouse to occupy the home along with a child or children of the family.[11]

---

[5] s.23(2) and the Matrimonial Homes (Family Protection) (Scotland) Act 1981 (Commencement) Order 1982 (S.I. 1982 No. 972).
[6] See paras. 3-06 to 3-21 below.
[7] Law Reform (Miscellaneous Provisions) (Scotland) Act 1985, s.13.
[8] See paras. 6-15 and 6-18 below.
[9] See para. 2-18 below.
[10] See para. 2-56 below.
[11] See para. 2-06 below.

1–07. There have been two major studies of the workings of the Act. The first, undertaken by the Institute of Housing and the Scottish Homeless Group, investigated the problems faced by local authority landlords and tenants as a result of marital breakdown and the way in which the Act operated in this area. A report was published in February 1985.[12] The second project, funded by the Scottish Home and Health Department, is being carried out by Dr Peter Robson, Marie Robertson and Alice Ann Jackson of the University of Strathclyde Law School. It is concerned with the granting of exclusion orders, matrimonial interdicts and powers of arrest. It focuses on the criteria which the courts use in operating the Act and the problems solicitors, their clients and the police encounter. This research is due to be completed and published by mid-1986. The findings in these studies could well lead to further changes being made to the Act.

---

[12] Institute of Housing and Scottish Homeless Group, *Housing and Marital Breakdown— The Local Authority Response,* Final Report published by the University of Strathclyde.

CHAPTER 2

OCCUPANCY OF THE MATRIMONIAL HOME

2–01. Introduction

Before the Act came into force a spouse who was the sole owner or tenant of the matrimonial home or other property was entitled to eject his or her spouse from it. The non-owner or tenant spouse was a precarious occupier whose occupancy depended upon the goodwill of the other spouse.[1] The first part of the Act, consisting of ss. 1 to 5, confers a statutory right of occupancy upon spouses not otherwise entitled to occupy the matrimonial home, together with various ancillary rights, and provides machinery for regulating the occupancy rights of either spouse. The previous law remains applicable to property other than a matrimonial home.

2–02. The statutory rights of occupancy of the matrimonial home arise by operation of law by virtue of the non-entitled spouse's status as a spouse. They are an incident of marriage. The position of unmarried but cohabiting couples is discussed later in Chapter 7.

2–03. Occupancy rights

The statutory occupancy rights conferred upon a non-entitled spouse[2] consist of first, the right, if in occupation, to continue to occupy the matrimonial home,[3] and, secondly, the right, if not in occupation, to enter into and occupy the matrimonial home.[4] Initially the formula for the first right was not to be excluded from the matrimonial home or any part of it by the entitled spouse. The present formula emphasises that the non-entitled spouse's right is not simply a personal right to live in the home but is a right to occupy it (which includes for example the right to invite visitors), in line with the second right. Section 1(4) provides that these rights are referred to as occupancy rights in the Act.[5] It has been argued,[6] on the basis of the original formulation, that where the phrase "occupancy rights" occurs elsewhere in the Act it means only the occupancy rights conferred on the spouse of a sole proprietor and not the rights of occupation which a proprietor has by virtue of his or her title or other entitlement to occupy property.

2–04. The change in the formulation of section 1(1)(a) would appear to remove one of the main planks of the argument. The rights in paragraphs (a) and (b) no longer contain a reference to an entitled spouse, so that it is no longer implied that the rights are only those of non-entitled spouses. The present rights are equally applicable to owners, tenants and other entitled

---

[1] *MacLure* v. *MacLure*, 1911 S.C. 200; *Millar* v. *Millar*, 1940 S.C. 56.
[2] A polygamous proprietor possesses a plurality of non-entitled spouses presenting problems aplenty!
[3] s.1(1)(a), as amended by the Law Reform (Miscellaneous Provisions) (Scotland) Act 1985, s.13(2).
[4] s.1(1)(b).
[5] See also s.22 in so far as spouses are concerned.
[6] G.L. Gretton, "The Matrimonial Homes (Family Protection) (Scotland) Act 1981: A Fundamental Difficulty," 1981 S.L.T. (News) 297.

spouses. The main provisions where the suggested restricted interpretation would have the most serious effects are in sections 3 and 4. These empower the courts to regulate and suspend a spouse's occupancy rights, and the Act would have almost completely failed in its purpose if only the occupancy rights of non-entitled spouses could be regulated or suspended. Section 3(1), however, confers a title on a spouse (whether non-entitled, entitled, or entitled with the other spouse) to apply to the court for orders enforcing or protecting his or her occupancy rights or regulating or restricting the occupancy rights of the other spouse. The context demands that "occupancy rights" includes rights flowing from title. Similarly, under section 4(1), where one spouse is entitled and the other is non-entitled or if both spouses are entitled, either spouse may apply for an order suspending the occupancy rights of the other. Since the spouse sought to be excluded can be entitled (either alone or with the applicant), it follows that the court must have power to suspend occupancy rights arising by virtue of a title. Finally, it is a rule of statutory interpretation that if the meaning of a word or phrase as defined in the statute leads, in the context of a particular provision, to an unreasonable result, the ordinary meaning may be substituted.[7] In connection with residential property the ordinary meaning of occupancy rights is simply the rights to occupy the property.

2–05. The phrases "if in occupation" and "if not in occupation" occur in the definition of statutory occupancy rights.[8] Clearly something different from actual residence is meant. It has been held in considering very similar provisions in the Matrimonial Homes Act 1967 (which applies to England and Wales) that a wife remained in occupation if she left some of her belongings in the home and intended to return to live there.[9]

2–06. The Law Society of Scotland, in their review of the working of the Act,[10] drew attention to the problem caused by the refusal by some husbands to allow the children of the marriage to occupy the matrimonial home. A refusal to allow the children to live at home effectively defeats the wife's statutory occupancy rights, since she will not wish to exercise them at the price of abandoning the children. To remedy this defect a new subsection was added[11] which provides that the statutory occupancy rights include the right of the non-entitled spouse to occupy and enter the matrimonial home together with any child of the family. It is not necessary that the spouse should have custody of the child or children.

2–07. "Child of the family" is defined in section 22, and has a much wider meaning than a child of the marriage. It includes a child or grandchild of either spouse, and any person who has been brought up and accepted by either spouse as if he or she were a child of that spouse. There is no limit on the age of a child, grandchild or person. Acceptance as a child of the family

---

[7] Craies, *Statute Law* (7th ed.), p. 101; *Strathearn* v. *Padden*, 1926 S.C. (J.) 9, *per* Lord Justice-General Clyde at p. 13.

[8] s.1(1)(*a*) and (*b*).

[9] *Hoggett* v. *Hoggett* (1979) 39 P. & C.R. 121. The Matrimonial Homes Act 1967 has been repealed and re-enacted by the Matrimonial Homes Act 1983, a consolidation measure.

[10] Council memorandum, "The Matrimonial Homes (Family Protection) (Scotland) Act 1981" (1984) 29 J.L.S. 75.

[11] s.1(1A), by s.13(3) of the Law Reform (Miscellaneous Provisions) (Scotland) Act 1985.

involves being regarded by the spouse as a permanent member of the family, as for example where a man brings up his deceased brother's orphaned children. An *au pair* or other long-stay visitors are not permanent while foster children are not normally regarded by foster-parents as members of their family.

2–08. Section 22 of the Rent (Scotland) Act 1984 provides that it is an offence for any person unlawfully to deprive residential occupiers of their occupation of premises or to harass them in an attempt to make them leave. A residential occupier includes a person occupying premises as a residence by virtue of any enactment. As a consequence of the Matrimonial Homes Act conferring statutory occupancy rights on non-entitled spouses, such spouses are residential occupiers within the meaning of the 1984 Act.

2–09. Entitled and non-entitled spouses

Section 1(1) confers occupancy rights upon a spouse who is not otherwise entitled or permitted to occupy the matrimonial home, provided the other spouse is so entitled or permitted. The entitled or permitted spouse is termed the entitled spouse while the other spouse, on whom statutory occupancy rights are conferred, is termed the non-entitled spouse. Spouses who share an entitlement or permission to occupy a matrimonial home are discussed later.[12] An entitled spouse includes a sole owner, whether by infeftment or a personal right, a sole tenant, a liferenter and a person who occupies by virtue of a permission from, for example, the trustees of a family settlement, his or her employer or a friend.

2–10. Incorporated bodies (such as the University of Aberdeen) obviously cannot be spouses or have spouses, non-entitled or otherwise. But doubts have arisen whether executors and other individuals[13] with title in a representative capacity are entitled spouses. It is suggested that they are not. Section 22 of the Act defines matrimonial home by reference to the concept of family residence. The right to occupy a matrimonial home is therefore a right to occupy it as a residence, rather than a right to occupy it for the purpose of executry administration[14] or realisation on behalf of creditors.

2–11. The granting of a permission to occupy the matrimonial home by an owner or tenant to his or her spouse does not prevent that spouse from becoming a non-entitled spouse and hence becoming vested with statutory occupancy rights and protected by the various provisions of the Act. Section 1(1) comes into operation if one spouse is "entitled or permitted by a third party" to occupy and the other spouse is not "so entitled or permitted." The word "so" governs both entitled and permitted, and, since the other spouse is permitted by the entitled spouse rather than a third party, he or she is not so permitted and is therefore a non-entitled spouse.

2–12. Section 1(2) deals with an uncommon situation where occupancy rights are not conferred upon the spouse of an entitled spouse. If an entitled spouse shares the entitlement or permission to occupy the matrimonial home

---

[12] para. 2-64 below.
[13] A bank acting as an executor clearly cannot be an entitled spouse!
[14] The Succession (Scotland) Act 1964, s.14(1) vests the deceased's heritable property in the executor for the purposes of administration.

with a third party (*i.e.* a person other than his or her spouse), the other spouse becomes a non-entitled spouse and hence acquires occupancy rights only if the third party has waived his or her right of occupation. The waiver need not be express; it could be implied from residence in another home. For example, if a married son and his mother are co-owners of the matrimonial home, the son's wife has no occupancy rights if the mother lives with them.[15] On the other hand if the mother lives elsewhere the son's wife comes within the protection of the Act. Homes with "granny flats" could cause problems where granny and one of the spouses are co-owners, though the pattern of family living is such that granny generally keeps to her own quarters. It might be advisable for the other spouse to seek an express waiver from granny of her right to occupy the main residence.

2–13. Matrimonial home

Occupancy rights and other rights conferred on spouses by the Act arise only in relation to a matrimonial home.[16] "Matrimonial home" is defined in section 22. It may be a detached house, a terraced house, a flat or part of a building occupied as a separate dwelling, a caravan (whether fixed or mobile), a house-boat or "other structure" such as a converted railway carriage or a tinker's tent. In the following discussion all these types of property are referred to as a house.

2–14. The matrimonial home is not just the house itself; it may include any garden or other ground or building. The definition is perhaps ambiguous as regards these additional items. On one reading the item must be *either* attached to and usually occupied with the house *or* attached to and otherwise required for the amenity or convenience of the house. The other interpretation is that the item must be *either* attached to and usually occupied with the house *or* otherwise required for the amenity and convenience of the house. Two items where the above interpretations produce different results are a discontiguous garage and an undivided share of the garden grounds in the centre of a square. The departmental practice of the Registers of Scotland is based on the second interpretation. In the case of an application for registration in the Land Register consequent upon the sale of a discontiguous garage, an assurance is required that the garage was not used as an adjunct of a matrimonial home. If such an assurance cannot be given then a consent, renunciation, affidavit, etc., must be presented before a statement that there are no subsisting occupancy rights can be inserted in the title sheet of the garage. Undivided shares of gardens are always regarded as adjuncts of homes.[17] The phrase "occupied with" must mean occupied by the entitled spouse as an adjunct of the family residence, otherwise the whole of the farmland attached to a matrimonial farmhouse would be included as part of the matrimonial home, which is clearly absurd.

2–15. The Act extends to Scotland only.[18] There is a strong presumption

---

[15] The mother and son would not need to obtain the wife's consent to any dealing affecting the home and could swear an affidavit that it was not a matrimonial home to which a spouse of the seller has occupancy rights. See para. 6-04 below.

[16] Occupancy rights can be renounced in a house which is to become a matrimonial home. See para. 2-60 below.

[17] Personal communication from the Keeper of the Registers of Scotland.

[18] s.23(3).

that legislation applying to immoveable property is territorial in operation.[19] The Act is therefore taken to apply only to houses situated in Scotland and not to property in England and Wales or foreign holiday homes.

2-16. A house is a matrimonial home if it "has been provided or has been made available by one or both of the spouses as, or has become, a family residence." The normal case of a matrimonial home is a house in which the spouses live, together with any children or other members of their family. Such a house has become a family residence. Once the house has become a family residence it does not cease to be a matrimonial home simply because both spouses cease to live together there.[20] Whether a house has become a family residence depends on whether the spouses have lived together in it and if so for how long. Residence denotes some degree of permanence in the living arrangements.[21] For example, if a wife owned a house in which her husband had only lived for a week or so in an unsuccessful attempt at reconciliation, her house would probably not become a matrimonial home.

2-17. From the fact that the definition of matrimonial home consists of two alternative parts, it can be deduced that the first alternative—"has been provided or has been made available . . . as a family residence"—covers a house which was intended to become a family residence but which never became one. For example, a wife may have acquired a cottage for herself and her husband to live in on their retirement, or a couple working abroad may acquire a house for themselves and their children to live in when they return to Scotland. These will be matrimonial homes even though neither spouse has ever lived there. It should be noted, however, that the spouse of the proprietor is a non-entitled spouse only if the proprietor is entitled to occupy the house.[22] Thus where the retirement cottage or future family home is let until it is required, the owner's spouse does not have any statutory occupancy rights in it during the period of the lease. Normally this will not matter as the owner and spouse are living elsewhere. However, the protection against sale or another dealing is framed with reference to a dealing of an entitled spouse.[23] It would be an absurd and surely unintended result if an entitled spouse could sell the matrimonial home against his or her spouse's will simply by letting it first.

2-18. Doubts have arisen whether a house acquired by a spouse after separation for his or her own occupation is a matrimonial home. Occupation by one person cannot turn a house into a family residence, but where the separated spouse has children of the family living there too, it could be argued that such a house is a family residence, the family consisting of the spouse and the children. Consideration of the social policy behind the Act suggests that a family means a family which includes both spouses, otherwise the effect would be to confer on a spouse occupancy rights in a house which the other had acquired for the express purpose of living a separate life. In

---

[19] Anton, *Private International Law,* p. 76; *British South Africa Co.* v. *Companhia de Moçambique* [1893] A.C. 602; *Hesperides Hotels Ltd.* v. *Muftizade* [1979] A.C. 508.
[20] See para. 2-52 *et seq.* below.
[21] The *Shorter Oxford English Dictionary* includes among the meanings of *reside,* "settle . . . dwell permanently or for a considerable time . . . have one's settled or usual abode."
[22] s.1(1).
[23] s.6(1).

order to clarify the position, section 13(10) of the Law Reform (Miscellaneous Provisions) (Scotland) Act 1985 was passed providing that a matrimonial home does not include a residence provided or made available "by one spouse for that spouse to reside in, whether with any child of the family or not, separately from the other spouse." While this amendment probably caters for the majority of the cases, it unfortunately does not deal with the case where a new house is provided by a spouse's parent or other member of his or her family. The social policy considerations referred to above ought to preclude the other spouse from acquiring occupancy rights. In order to avoid doubts, the spouse's parent or other relative would be well advised to provide the spouse with money to acquire a new home rather than provide the home itself.

2–19. On separation, one spouse may provide a house for the other spouse to live in together with any children. Such a house is not a matrimonial home[24] and the rights of the occupying spouse depend on the terms on which the accommodation was provided.

2–20. It is possible for a married couple to possess more than one matrimonial home. They may have two houses which they use as family residences or a main residence in a cottage or residential caravan which they use regularly for holidays or at weekends. In order to qualify as a matrimonial home, holiday accommodation must have more than occasional use, since residence carries the connotation of settled abode.[25]

2–21. Once a house has become a matrimonial home it does not cease to be so simply because one or both spouses live elsewhere. The question of cessation is best considered in relation to termination of the non-entitled spouse's occupancy rights discussed in paragraphs 2-52 to 2-58 below.

2–22. Subsidiary rights exercisable

In order to protect or preserve his or her occupancy rights a non-entitled spouse may exercise certain subsidiary rights in relation to the matrimonial home. These rights may be exercised without having to apply to the court or obtain the consent of the entitled spouse. They comprise:

(1) Payment of outgoings due by the entitled spouse such as rent, rates and secured loan instalments.[26] This right is strictly speaking unnecessary, as under the common law a debt may be paid by a person other than the debtor.[27] A good faith heritable creditor may apply to the court for an order requiring a resident non-entitled spouse to pay sums due by the absent entitled spouse under the security.[28]

(2) Performance of obligations due by the entitled spouse,[29] such as paying for work already carried out on the home or erecting a wall around the feu in accordance with conditions in the feu charter. Personal obligations of the

---

[24] *McRobbie* v. *McRobbie*, Outer House, 3 Aug. 1983 (unreported but noted in (1984) 29 J.L.S. 5).
[25] See n.21 to para. 2-16 above.
[26] s.2(1)(*a*).
[27] Bell, *Prin.* (4th ed.), s. 557.
[28] s.8(1). See para. 6-18 below.
[29] s.2(1)(*b*).

entitled spouse unrelated to the matrimonial home and obligations relating to non-essential repairs or improvements are excluded.[30]

(3) Enforcement of obligations due to the entitled spouse,[31] such as an obligation by the landlord to keep in repair the structure and exterior of the matrimonial home.[32] The non-entitled spouse has no standing to enforce obligations unconnected with the matrimonial home.

(4) Carrying out such essential repairs to the home as the entitled spouse could carry out.[33] Essential repairs are those which are necessary to enable the home to be used as a residence, such as mending a leaking roof or burst water-pipes. Works required to bring the home up to a tolerable standard[34] would normally be classed as improvements rather than repairs. Redecoration is maintenance or improvement rather than repair, and furthermore would not usually be regarded as essential.[35] Although the eradication of dry rot would be classed as an essential repair, it would be prudent in view of the cost and scale of the work usually involved to apply to the court for authority if the entitled spouse refuses to agree to it being carried out.

(5) Taking such other steps to protect occupancy rights as the entitled spouse could take to protect his or her occupancy rights.[36] By analogy with a tenant, a non-entitled spouse has a title at common law to institute or defend proceedings to protect his or her occupancy rights.[37] The above provision confers a statutory title on the non-entitled spouse. But the statutory title may be narrower in scope, as any such steps undertaken by virtue of it must be for "the purpose of securing" the non-entitled spouse's occupancy rights.[38] This could be construed as limiting any steps to those necessary to preserve the existing situation. On this view the non-entitled spouse would have a statutory title to defend an action of removing brought by the landlord but not to apply for determination of a fair rent,[39] while the competence of instituting proceedings to abate a nuisance would depend on whether the nuisance was new or existing. A non-entitled spouse may fail to take the necessary steps through ignorance of third-party proceedings against the entitled spouse, because there is no requirement to intimate such proceedings to non-entitled spouses.

2–23. Any payment made or obligation performed by a non-entitled spouse is deemed, as far as third parties are concerned, to be a payment or performance by the entitled spouse. Likewise an obligation enforced by a non-entitled spouse is treated as having been enforced by the entitled spouse.[40]

2–24. Broadly similar rights may be exercised by a non-owner spouse in relation to furniture and plenishings owned by the other spouse.[41]

[30] s.2(1)(*b*).
[31] s.2(1)(*c*).
[32] Housing (Scotland) Act 1966, s.8.
[33] s.2(1)(*d*),
[34] Housing (Scotland) Act 1974, s.14.
[35] An application may be made to the court in respect of improvements and non-essential repairs: see para. 2-25 below.
[36] s.2(1)(*f*).
[37] See para. 2-50 and n. 86 below.
[38] s.2(1).
[39] Rent (Scotland) Act 1984, s. 46; application to be made by landlord or tenant.
[40] s.2(2).
[41] s.2(5)(*a*).

2–25. Authorisation of non-essential repairs

Paragraph (*e*) of section 2(1) empowers the court, on an application by the non-entitled spouse, to grant authority for non-essential repairs or improvements to be carried out on the matrimonial home where the entitled spouse does not consent to the work. The court must under this paragraph consider the work to be appropriate for the reasonable enjoyment of occupancy rights. It has been pointed out[42] that it is difficult to square this power to authorise improvements with the opening words of section 2(1), which provide that the various rights are for "the purpose of securing the occupancy rights" of the non-entitled spouse. Securing suggests maintaining the existing condition of the home rather than improving it, and on this view the court's power is limited to items such as minor improvements made in the course of essential repairs or redecoration to make good deterioration.

2–26. Apportionment of expenditure between spouses

The Act empowers the court on application by either spouse to apportion certain items of expenditure incurred in relation to a matrimonial home and its furniture and plenishings between the spouses. The existing common law remedies for the recovery of such expenditure, based on loan, repetition and recompense, often fail to provide an equitable solution.[43] Where one spouse claims that he or she in spending money on the home was lending it to the other, proof of loan is limited to the other spouse's writ or oath. Such proof is generally not available. Repetition and recompense would normally be applicable only if the person incurring the expenditure does so in the (erroneous) belief that he or she had, or would acquire, an interest in the house. In the vast majority of cases involving married couples there is no error, with the result that the expenditure is regarded as having been made for the benefit of the person making it[44] and is therefore not recoverable from the other spouse.

2–27. Where one spouse is entitled and the other spouse is non-entitled, either may apply to the court under section 2(3) for an order apportioning between them expenditure incurred or to be incurred on their matrimonial home. Apportionment of future expenditure could be useful in connection with the running costs of the home owned or tenanted by one spouse but occupied by the other. Another use might be to ascertain the extent of each spouse's liability for the cost of expensive repairs before instructing the work to be carried out. Where the expenditure is incurred (or is to be incurred) by one spouse without the consent of the other, the court's power of apportionment is limited to the outgoings of the home and the cost of essential repairs.[45] If, however, the expenditure was or is consented to, the court can apportion any expenditure incurred in relation to the matrimonial home.[46] The scope of this new power is very wide. Under the common law a

---

[42] Clive, *Husband and Wife* (2nd ed.), p. 714.
[43] Clive, *op. cit.*, pp. 318-320.
[44] As the Scottish Law Commission observed in recommending apportionment such an assumption is unrealistic. "Expenditure incurred on a matrimonial home during the subsistence of a marriage may be made by one spouse or the other purely as a matter of convenience; and such expenditure is made not for the benefit of one spouse, but for the benefit of both": Scot. Law Com. No. 60, para. 2.65.
[45] s.2(3)(*a*), applying s.2(1)(*a*) and (*d*).
[46] s.2(3)(*b*).

spouse who contributed to the purchase price of a home the title to which is taken in the other spouse's name will neither obtain an interest in the property nor be able to recover the money.[47] The new power of apportionment will at least enable the contribution or part of it to be recovered. The court's powers can be exercised only in relation to expenditure of money; it cannot order payment to a spouse who has expended time and skill on DIY repairs or improvements.[48]

2–28. Similar powers of apportionment exist in relation to expenditure incurred on furniture and plenishings in the home.[49] Any application to the court for apportionment of expenditure on either the matrimonial home or its furniture and plenishings must be made within five years of the date on which the expenditure was incurred.[50] In implement of its apportionment order the court may grant a decree for payment of money by one spouse to the other.[51]

2–29. Regulation of occupancy rights by court
Both spouses have as a result of the Act occupancy rights in relation to their matrimonial home. Provision therefore requires to be made for regulating these rights in the event of a dispute between the spouses. Section 3(1) sets out the types of orders which may be made.

2–30. *Declaring occupancy rights.* Either spouse may apply to the court for a declarator[52] that he or she has occupancy rights in relation to the house in question. It was envisaged that this procedure would serve as a way of determining whether a particular property was a matrimonial home, since the court is directed to grant the application if it is satisfied that the property is a matrimonial home.[53] In practice, however, it appears to be regarded as a convenient peg on which to hang other applications, such as for exclusion of the other spouse.[54]

2–31. *Enforcing occupancy rights.* The court may make an order enforcing the occupancy rights of the applicant spouse. Such an order would be needed where the applicant spouse has been put out or locked out of the matrimonial home by the other spouse and wishes to return to it. Another provision which has a bearing on this matter is section 1(3), and it is convenient to discuss it in the context of enforcement.

2–32. Section 1(3) provides that where an entitled spouse refuses to allow the other spouse (*i.e.* the non-entitled spouse) to exercise the right to enter into and occupy the home, the non-entitled spouse may do so only with the leave of the court granted under section 3(3) or (4).[55] It is clear that the

---

[47] See para. 2-26 above.
[48] These factors can be taken into account by a court in making orders for financial provision on granting decree of divorce or nullity: Family Law (Scotland) Act 1985, s.9.
[49] s.2(5)(*b*).
[50] s.2(7).
[51] s.2(6).
[52] s.3(1)(*a*); *McRobbie* v. *McRobbie,* Outer House, 3 Aug. 1983 (unreported but noted in (1984) 29 J.L.S. 5).
[53] s.3(3).
[54] *Bell* v. *Bell,* 1982 S.L.T. 518 (declarator sought by non-entitled spouse); *Brown* v. *Brown,* 1985 S.L.T. 376 (declarator sought by sole tenant).
[55] s.3(4) deals with interim orders; see para. 2-46 below.

only competent way by which a non-entitled spouse not in occupation[56] can enforce his or her occupancy rights is by an application under section 3(1)(*b*). What is less clear is the competence in other cases—a non-entitled spouse in occupation but not in residence, or an entitled spouse whether or not in occupation—of proceedings to enforce occupancy rights otherwise than by means of an application under section 3(1)(*b*). On the one hand, the limited terms of section 1(3) suggest that other proceedings are not excluded for these cases. On the other hand, section 3(1) applies to any spouse, whether entitled, non-entitled or sharing title. A distinction may perhaps be drawn between non-entitled and entitled spouses. In the former case the right to occupy and the remedies are, if not given in the same breath, at least conferred by the same statute. The presumption is that only the statutory remedy can be used.[57] In the latter case the rights of entitled spouses to occupy stem from their title, and various remedies were available prior to the Act for the enforcement of these occupancy rights. These existing remedies remain in the absence of any express provision or necessary implication in the Act to the contrary.[58]

2–33. In dealing with an application under paragraphs (*b*) to (*e*) of section 3(1) the court may make such order as seems just and reasonable having regard to all the circumstances of the case and in particular to the spouses' needs, resources and conduct, the needs of any child of the family, any business use of the home and whether the entitled spouse has offered the non-entitled spouse suitable alternative accommodation.[59] These guidelines would apply to an application by a non-entitled spouse not in occupation seeking to re-enter the matrimonial home against the wishes of the entitled spouse,[60] but it is not clear whether they also apply in other cases where proceedings are brought to enforce occupancy rights. For example, has the court a discretion to enforce the occupancy rights of an owner or tenant who wishes to return to live in the home? The fact that under section 1(3) it is only a non-entitled spouse not in occupation who has to seek the leave of the court suggests that such a spouse's rights are in some way less than the occupancy rights of other spouses. But it could be argued that any proceedings to enforce occupancy rights are, in substance if not in form, an application under section 3(1)(*b*). While it would be sensible to apply the same guidelines to all types of proceedings the point must await clarification.

2–34. The enforcement of occupancy rights and exclusion are closely connected, for a refusal to grant an application for enforcement of a non-resident applicant's occupancy rights is tantamount to excluding him or her. While section 3(5) prevents the court from granting an order under section 3(3) which would have the effect of excluding the non-applicant spouse, it does not prevent the granting of an order which has the effect of excluding the applicant spouse. There is much to be said on a commonsense basis for

---

[56] See para. 2-05 above for the meaning of "not in occupation."
[57] Craies, *Statute Law* (7th ed.), pp. 247-248; *Barraclough* v. *Brown* [1897] A.C. 615; *Wilkinson* v. *Barking Corporation* [1948] 1 K.B. 721.
[58] Craies, *op. cit.*, pp. 344-345; *Great Northern Fishing Co.* v. *Edgehill* (1883) 11 Q.B.D. 225, at p. 226.
[59] s.3(3).
[60] *Nimmo* v. *Nimmo*, Glasgow Sheriff Court, 12 Aug. 1983 (reported in (1984) 29 J.L.S. 4).

making the criteria for refusing an application for enforcement of occupancy rights (where the purpose of the application is to re-enter the home) the same as the stringent criteria for granting an exclusion order.[61] The use of different criteria encourages people to resort to self-help by putting their spouse out of the home. Given the different criteria in sections 3 and 4 of the Act, it does not seem possible to adopt such an approach.

2–35. *Restricting occupancy rights.* Under section 3(1)(c) the court is empowered on application by one spouse to restrict the occupancy rights of the other. Such an order might be sought to prevent the other spouse from inviting people to stay in the matrimonial home (such as lodgers, lovers or in-laws) whose presence would adversely affect the applicant's occupancy rights.[62] Section 3(5) prevents a restriction order which amounts to exclusion from the matrimonial home being granted. The purpose of this rule is to prevent the stringent criteria for exclusion orders[63] being sidestepped. It would be in accord with the spirit of the legislation if it was incompetent to grant a restriction order having the effect of excluding a spouse from the residential part of a matrimonial home used both as a residence and business premises (such as a dentist's surgery).

2–36. *Regulating occupancy rights.* The court may on an application made by a spouse regulate the occupancy rights of either spouse.[64] There is a considerable overlap between regulation and restriction, since regulation usually involves some elements of restriction. Combined regulation and restriction orders could be useful where the matrimonial home is so constructed as to make it possible to allocate separate accommodation to each of the spouses.[65]

2–37. *Protecting occupancy rights.* Section 3(1)(e) empowers the court to make an order protecting the occupancy rights of the applicant spouse. Such an order might take the form of an interdict prohibiting a "lock-out" or harassment designed to make the applicant leave. Orders under this paragraph can only be granted against the other spouse, or those authorised by him or her, since the court's powers are limited to protecting the applicant's rights "in relation to the other spouse." But the court has power at common law to grant an order protecting occupancy rights against wrongful actions or threatened actions of third parties.

2–38. Use and possession of furniture and plenishings
To supplement rights of occupancy a spouse may acquire the right to use and possess furniture and plenishings owned, hired or being acquired under a hire-purchase or conditional sale agreement by the other spouse. This right does not arise by operation of law; an application has to be made to the court under section 3(2). The need for such orders should be reduced after the coming into force of section 25 of the Family Law (Scotland) Act 1985

---

[61] s.4. See Chap. 3.
[62] Where the entitled spouse confers a right on a third party (by letting a room for example) rather than a permission or an invitation this constitutes a dealing. See Chap. 6.
[63] s.4(2) and (3).
[64] s.3(1)(d).
[65] These orders were dubbed "the west wing solution" in the Commons committee stage debates. Few local authority houses possess west wings!

which provides that household goods kept or used in the matrimonial home for the joint domestic purposes of the spouses are presumed to be owned in common.

2–39.   It is a condition of competence of an application under section 3(2) that the applicant has occupancy rights in the matrimonial home in which the items are situated. Occupancy rights is probably meant in the broad sense of rights of occupancy arising from title or conferred by the Act, since the section refers to one spouse and the other spouse instead of entitled and non-entitled spouses. Another requirement is that the applicant has not renounced his or her right to make such an application.[66] The furniture and plenishings in respect of which use and possession is sought must be situated in the matrimonial home at the time of the application.

2–40.   Furniture and plenishings comprise articles which are reasonably necessary to enable the home to be used as a family residence.[67] Tables, chairs, sofas, beds and bedding, wardrobes, chests, carpets, curtains, fires, cookers, fridges and other normal household appliances would all be regarded as furniture and plenishings. But clothes, personal effects and items used for business or leisure would not be so regarded. The position of items such as books, pictures or a piano would depend on their value, the standard of furnishing and each spouse's particular need for such items. As the matrimonial home includes the garden and garage, lawnmowers and tools could also count as furniture and plenishings. It should be noted that a use and possession order may not be made in relation to a car or a caravan.[68]

2–41.   In deciding an application for a use and possession order the court is directed to make such order as seems to be just and reasonable. It is required to have regard to all the circumstances of the case, and in particular to the needs, resources and conduct of the spouses, the needs of any child of the family, any business use of the home or the furniture and plenishings, and whether the entitled spouse has offered the non-entitled spouse suitable alternative accommodation.[69] The court may limit use and possession to items specified in the order instead of granting an application in respect of all the furniture and plenishings.

2–42.   A use and possession order confers a right to use and possess only in the matrimonial home. The user may not remove them from there. It is not clear whether an order confers sole use and possession on the applicant or whether he or she becomes a joint owner and possessor along with the owner or hirer spouse. The point is perhaps of no great practical significance, because a use and possession order will normally not be sought where the couple are living together. An order does not affect ownership; it neither divests the owner or hirer of his or her title, nor does it confer a title on the applicant spouse.[70] The owner or hirer can however be interdicted from

---

[66] s.3(8).
[67] s.22.
[68] s.22. The caravan might be a matrimonial home if it was used as family residence by another couple.
[69] s.3(3)(*a*)-(*e*).
[70] s.2(5)(*a*) confers limited powers of management on the applicant spouse.

dealing with the items so as to defeat the orders, for example by removing them or selling them.[71] The power of the court to make "such order" as seems just and reasonable on granting the application for a use and possession order[72] implies a power to make ancillary orders and interdicts necessary to make the principal order effective. Apart from the statutory power, the court has a common law power to interdict a threatened legal wrong. Where removal is feared it would be prudent to apply for an interdict at the same time as applying for the use and possession order.[73]

2–43. A use and possession order does not affect the rights of third parties to the items in question. Thus the items may be repossessed by the hirer or hire-purchase company on default, or sold by virtue of a poinding for the debts of the owner spouse, unless the poinding is contrived.[74]

2–44. Continuation of tenancy

A statutory tenancy of a dwellinghouse under section 3 of the Rent (Scotland) Act 1984 continues so long as the tenant retains possession. In *Temple* v. *Mitchell*[75] it was held that the tenancy had terminated where the tenant abandoned his wife in the home and had no intention of returning there. Section 2(8) of the Act provides that such a tenancy is continued by possession by the spouse of the tenant. This section is not restricted to statutory tenancies; it could be of assistance where a contractual tenancy stipulated for termination if the tenant abandoned possession. The legislation dealing with security of tenure in the public sector already contains similar protection for deserted spouses. Thus a local authority landlord can recover possession by application to the court if the tenant and his or her spouse are absent from the house for the required period.[76] Similarly, before the procedure for repossession by notice can be used the house must be unoccupied.[77]

2–45. Continuation of the tenancy will cease on the termination of the marriage as the spouse of the tenant ceases to be a non-entitled spouse. This is a factor that may require to be borne in mind in deciding whether to bring an action of divorce or annulment.

2–46. Interim orders

While an application for orders relating to occupancy rights or use and possession of furniture and plenishings is pending, the court may, on application, grant interim orders. Notwithstanding the wide powers conferred by section 3(4) to make such interim orders as it may consider necessary or expedient, the court is impliedly restricted to interim orders of a similar nature to final orders or to orders it could have made under the law before the Act which remains competent. An interim order, like a final order, cannot be made to the effect of excluding a spouse from the matrimonial home.[78]

[71] He or she may also be liable to pay compensation or damages. See para. 2-48 below.
[72] s.3(3).
[73] See para. 2-47 below.
[74] s.11.
[75] 1956 S.C. 267, construing the same provision in s.15(1) of the Increase of Rent and Mortgage Interest (Restrictions) Act 1920.
[76] Tenants' Rights, Etc. (Scotland) Act 1980, Sched. 2, Pt. I, para. 5.
[77] 1980 Act, s.18(1).
[78] s.3(5).

2–47. An interim order can be made only if the spouse of the applicant has been notified of the application and been given an opportunity to appear.[79] In the Court of Session at least seven days' notice must be given,[80] but in the sheriff court, although most applications are deal with as ordinary causes[81] (where the period of notice is 14 days unless shortened), applications for interim orders are heard as soon as convenient. At first sight the requirement of prior notice seems to prevent the court from granting an immediate interim interdict against ejection of the applicant or interference with the furniture, plenishings and personal effects in the home, pending the determination of an application for a final order. The courts' jurisdiction to grant interdict is not removed by a statute except by clear language.[82] As the Act does not rule out the use of interdict, the common law remedy of an immediate interim interdict preventing alteration of the existing situation pending proceedings[83] remains available to protect applicants at the initial stages when protection is often most needed.[84]

2–48. Compensation for loss of occupancy or use and possession

Section 3(7) provides for an award of compensation to be paid to a non-entitled spouse, or owner in the case of furniture and plenishings, for any loss or impairment of his or her rights to occupy the matrimonial home or use and possess the furniture and plenishings. Compensation is available only where the act or default leading to the loss or impairment was that of the entitled spouse. Furthermore, that spouse must have intended the act or default to lead to the loss or impairment. For example, a wife whose husband maliciously cut off the water supply or smashed the windows would be entitled to claim compensation from him. Intention is a more severe criterion than foreseeability and could be difficult to establish. In the case of a wife who fails to pay the rent for the matrimonial home and as a result she and her husband are ejected, compensation would not be claimable if her failure to pay was due to lack of money, since the ejection, though a foreseeable result of failure to pay, was not the intended result.

2–49. Compensation is only available to a non-entitled spouse. The reason for this is that the entitled spouse can claim damages at common law for any damage done to the home and for any loss or impairment of his or her occupancy rights. Can a non-entitled spouse claim damages, or does the existence of the remedy of compensation preclude him or her from bringing an action of damages? It is thought that where both remedies would be available, the effect of section 3(7) is to make a claim for compensation the only competent remedy, because where a statute confers a new right and provides a remedy in relation to it, the statutory remedy alone is competent.[85]

[79] s.3(4).
[80] Rule of Court 188D(9), unless the court orders a lesser period of notice.
[81] Act of Sederunt (Applications under the Matrimonial Homes (Family Protection) (Scotland) Act 1981) 1982, r. 5.
[82] *Norfor* v. *Aberdeenshire Education Authority,* 1923 S.C. 881, *per* Lord Hunter at p. 888.
[83] *Affleck* v. *Affleck* (1862) 24 D. 291.
[84] W.J. Stewart, "Protecting the Furniture," 1984 S.L.T. (News) 301.
[85] *Barraclough* v. *Brown* [1897] A.C. 615. The courts' power to grant interdict can only be removed by clear language, but interdict is not relevant here.

2–50. A non-entitled spouse cannot, in terms of section 3(7), claim compensation where the act or default resulting in loss or impairment of occupancy rights is that of a third party. An example would be where a lorry crashes into the house through negligence on the part of the driver. In this situation, can the non-entitled spouse claim damages? He or she has an interest but there may be no statutory title to sue. Section 2(1)(*e*) may not confer a statutory title, since suing for damages after a loss of occupancy rights has occurred is perhaps not a step taken for the purpose of securing or protecting the rights. However, if, as seems reasonable, occupancy rights can be equiparated with tenancy, a non-entitled spouse would have a good common law title.[86] An alternative view would be that section 3(7) intended to exclude actions of damages by non-entitled spouses in all cases. Total exclusion would not leave the non-entitled spouse without a remedy, for if the entitled spouse failed to sue for damages and make good the property, that would amount to a deliberate default which would ground a claim for compensation. This seems convoluted and the better view would seem to be that a non-entitled spouse has a direct right to claim damages in cases where a claim for compensation under section 3(7) cannot be made.

2–51. The use of the word "compensation," together with the court's duty to award such compensation as it considers just and reasonable in all the circumstances, suggests that the amount of compensation will be assessed in a different way from damages. It should be noted that section 2(2) of the Law Reform (Husband and Wife) Act 1962, which empowers the court to dismiss an action if no substantial benefit would accrue to either spouse, does not apply to an action for compensation.[87]

2–52. Termination of statutory occupancy rights
The Act does not state explicitly in what circumstances the occupancy rights conferred on non-entitled spouses terminate. Apart from renunciation (see paragraphs 2-59 to 2-63 below), it can be inferred that occupancy rights come to an end:
 (1) on termination of the marriage;
 (2) on the entitled spouse ceasing to be entitled;
 (3) by prescription;
 (4) by non-exercise for five years after disposal of the home;
 (5) on the non-entitled spouse ceasing to be non-entitled; and
 (6) on destruction of the matrimonial home.

2–53. As section 1(1) confers occupancy rights upon the spouse of a proprietor, it is implicit that these rights terminate on the death of either spouse or on the dissolution of the marriage by divorce or annulment.[88] Consistent with this analysis, any court order under section 3 or 4 regulating

---

[86] "In the case of more permanent injuries there has never been any doubt of an occupying tenant's title to sue for declarator, damages, interdict, removing or restitution in so far as his interest exists or otherwise to protect his holding": Rankine, *The Law of Leases in Scotland* (3rd ed.), p. 710.
[87] s.21, and see para. 8-04 below.
[88] But see para. 2-65 below for the court's powers under the Family Law (Scotland) Act 1985.

or suspending occupancy rights terminates automatically on the termination of the marriage.[89]

2–54.   On the cessation of the entitled spouse's entitlement to occupy the matrimonial home, the non-entitled spouse's occupancy rights also terminate, subject to provisions protecting them from dealings[90] or contrivances.[91] This is because a non-entitled spouse is defined in section 1(1) as the spouse of an entitled spouse. An entitled spouse may lose his or her entitlement to occupy as the result of a termination or withdrawal of permission by a third party (the employer of a service occupant, for example), sequestration,[92] compulsory acquisition, a sale or lease by a heritable creditor in the exercise of powers under the security, or a disposal of the home in accordance with the provisions of sections 6 and 7 of the Act. A court order under section 3 or 4 regulating or suspending occupancy rights ceases to have effect on the cessation of the entitled spouse's entitlement.[93]

2–55.   Under section 8 of the Prescription and Limitation (Scotland) Act 1973, a right relating to property is extinguished if it is not exercised or enforced for a continuous period of 20 years without any relevant claim having been made, unless it is imprescriptible. Schedule 3 to the 1973 Act lists the categories of imprescriptible rights; the only one that would include the right of a non-entitled spouse, if not in occupation, to enter into and occupy the home is "any right exercisable as a *res merae facultatis*."[94] It has been suggested that because the non-entitled spouse's right is not absolute, in that it requires the leave of the court if the entitled spouse refuses to allow the non-entitled spouse to enter,[95] the right is not a *res merae facultatis*.[96]

2–56.   In order to protect third-party occupants of the home against the possibility of a non-entitled spouse claiming occupancy rights many years after they took up occupation, section 6(3)(*f*)[97] provides that if after the entitled spouse has permanently ceased to be entitled to occupy the home, the non-entitled spouse has not occupied it at any time during a continuous period of five years, the occupancy rights are extinguished. This provision is discussed further in paragraph 6-17 below.

2–57.   A non-entitled spouse may cease to be non-entitled by becoming an entitled spouse. This could happen, for example, as the result of a transfer of the tenancy or ownership of the matrimonial home to the non-entitled spouse, or by both spouses becoming owners or tenants in common. A non-entitled spouse does not cease to be non-entitled simply by virtue of a permission to occupy granted by the entitled spouse.[98]

---

[89] s.5(1)(*a*).
[90] ss. 6-9, and see Chap. 6 below.
[91] s.12 and Bankruptcy (Scotland) Act 1985, s. 41. See para. 6-21 below.
[92] But the Bankruptcy (Scotland) Act 1985, s. 40, limits the trustee's power to sell the bankrupt's residence; see para. 6-19 below.
[93] s.5(1)(*b*).
[94] para. (*c*).
[95] s.1(3).
[96] Clive, *Husband and Wife* (2nd ed.), pp. 712-713.
[97] Added by Law Reform (Miscellaneous Provisions) (Scotland) Act 1985, s.13(6)(*c*).
[98] See para. 2-11 above.

2–58. Where a matrimonial home is totally destroyed the non-entitled spouse's occupancy rights cease.[99] It would depend on the circumstances and the intention of the entitled spouse whether any new building was a new matrimonial home. Another example of termination would be the removal of a matrimonial caravan, houseboat or tinker's tent to another country which did not have any laws conferring occupancy rights!

2–59. Renunciation of occupancy rights

Statutory occupancy rights may be renounced. Section 1(5) provides that a non-entitled spouse may renounce in writing his or her occupancy rights only in a particular matrimonial home or a particular property which is intended to be a matrimonial home. The intention was probably to make only written renunciations competent, but it is doubtful whether oral renunciations are excluded. The rule that where a statute provides that X may be done it means that only X is competent and that other methods of proceeding are incompetent applies where new statutory powers are conferred.[1] A right to renounce is, however, a well recognised legal right which can be exercised in writing or orally. While it is most unlikely that any person proposing to deal with an entitled spouse would be willing to settle the transaction on the basis of an oral renunciation, an oral renunciation might be founded on in court proceedings.

2–60. At first sight paragraph (b) seems contradictory. It may be asked how there can be a non-entitled spouse in property which is an intended matrimonial home rather than an actual matrimonial home. The intention is clear—to permit renunciation in advance of acquisition. This could be a useful facility where, for example, the wife's parents were willing to buy her a home only if her husband renounced his future occupancy rights beforehand. It is necessary to give meaning to this paragraph to regard "non-entitled spouse" as a label indicating the spouse who but for the renunciation would acquire statutory occupancy rights in the future.[2]

2–61. An engaged couple may wish to regulate their future occupancy rights in any home they acquire during their marriage. It would seem that each may make a general renunciation that would have effect in relation to a particular matrimonial home as and when one of the couple becomes an entitled spouse. While it may be necessary to read "non-entitled spouse" as a spouse who will become non-entitled to make sense of section 1(5), it is not necessary to read "spouse" as including a person who will become a spouse at some time in the future.

2–62. Section 1(6) contains further provisions relating to renunciations. To ensure that they are not entered into lightly the person renouncing has to swear or affirm before a notary public that the renunciation is made freely and without coercion of any kind. The notary should not, if at all possible, be the entitled spouse's solicitor or even a member of the same firm, to avoid any challenge on the ground of interest. The notary should make sure that the

---

[99] *Cantors Properties (Scotland) Ltd.* v. *Swears & Wells Ltd.,* 1977 S.L.T. (Notes) 30 (termination of a tenancy following destruction).
[1] Craies, *Statute Law* (7th ed.), pp. 286–287.
[2] A similar point arises in relation to s.6(3)(a)(i); see para. 6–08 below.

person renouncing has at least a general idea of the effects of the renunciation. If the renunciation is to be signed in a country other than Scotland, the oath or affirmation may be taken by any person authorised by the law of that country to administer oaths[3] or by the British ambassador, consul, etc.[4]

2–63. A spouse who renounces his or her occupancy rights is not protected against dealings relating to the matrimonial home[5] and is not entitled to apply for a use and possession order in relation to furniture and plenishings in the home.[6] Although such a spouse remains a non-entitled spouse and therefore is still entitled to apply for an order regulating occupancy or excluding the other spouse, the court would dismiss such an application on the ground of lack of interest. Moreover, if any order were to be granted the entitled spouse could immediately eject the non-entitled spouse thus rendering the order pointless. These considerations may not apply to an application for a tenancy transfer order,[7] for the effect would be to convert the renouncer into an entitled spouse. A matrimonial interdict with a power of arrest attached (prohibiting violence, for example) could competently be granted in favour of a spouse who had renounced, since section 14(2)(a) refers simply to spouses.

2–64. Both spouses entitled

Many couples nowadays own or rent their matrimonial home in common. It is likely that the Act has increased the number so doing. In these cases both spouses are entitled and have an equal right to occupy by virtue of their shared title. It would be possible for one spouse to be entitled or permitted in a different way from the other, although it is hard to envisage circumstances that are likely to arise in practice which would produce such an effect. Where both spouses are entitled the Act confers neither statutory occupancy rights nor any of the subsidiary rights on either spouse. In order to place such couples in as nearly the same position as couples where one of the spouses is entitled and the other non-entitled, the Act provides that either spouse may apply for orders regulating occupancy,[8] excluding the other entitled spouse,[9] authorising non-essential repairs and improvements,[10] or apportioning expenditure on the home between the spouses.[11]

2–65. Post-divorce occupancy rights

As mentioned above,[12] the statutory occupancy rights conferred on a non-entitled spouse by the Act cease on the dissolution of the marriage by divorce or annulment. However, section 14(2)(d) of the Family Law (Scotland) Act 1985 empowers the court, on or after granting decree of divorce or nullity,[13]

---

[3] Added to s.1(6) by the Law Reform (Miscellaneous Provisions) (Scotland) Act 1985, s.13(4).
[4] Commissioners for Oaths Act 1889, s.6.
[5] s.6(3)(a)(ii).
[6] s.3(2).
[7] Under s.13.
[8] s.3(1), (3) and (4).
[9] s.4.
[10] s.2(4)(a).
[11] s.2(4)(b).
[12] At para. 2-53.
[13] 1985 Act, s.17. For overseas divorces and annulments see the Matrimonial and Family Proceedings Act 1984, ss. 28 to 31.

to make an order regulating occupancy of the former matrimonial home or use and possession of the furniture and plenishings. The power to regulate occupancy includes a power to exclude one of the former spouses from the home. While an order is in effect, the person in whose favour it is granted can exercise the subsidiary rights contained in section 2 of the Act.[14] But he or she is not protected against dealings by sections 6 to 9 of the Act. Instead, the court may interdict any dealings, grant warrant to inhibit the proprietor or make any other ancillary order expedient to ensure that the occupancy right is not defeated.[15] Contrived adjudications, sequestrations or poindings can be recalled or annulled.[16]

[14] 1985 Act, s.14(5).
[15] 1985 Act, s.14(2)(*k*).
[16] 1985 Act, s.14(5).

CHAPTER 3

EXCLUSION ORDERS

3–01. Introduction

An exclusion order is an order of the court suspending a spouse's rights to occupy (by title or under the Act) the matrimonial home. Taken together with an interdict prohibiting that spouse from entering the home, it has the effect of excluding him or her from it. The purpose of exclusion orders is to provide victims of domestic violence (usually women) with an alternative to fleeing from their homes; the alternative being to have the perpetrators of the violence (usually men) excluded, thus leaving the victim in peaceful occupation of the home. This chapter is concerned with exclusion of spouses. Exclusion of cohabitees is dealt with in Chapter 7.

3–02. Not surprisingly the provisions on exclusion orders have proved the most controversial part of the Act and have been the most litigated. The first cases, *Bell* v. *Bell*[1] and *Smith* v. *Smith*,[2] adopted (in the eyes of those who welcomed the legislation) a very restrictive interpretation and calls were made in Parliament for urgent amending legislation. The courts in later cases have adopted a more liberal approach, but the possibility of further legislation after a research project funded by the Scottish Home and Health Department[3] has been completed, remains.

3–03. While an exclusion order suspends a person's occupancy rights, it does not affect other rights flowing from his or her title or conferred by the Act. For example, an excluded owner retains title to sue in respect of damage done to the property by the other spouse or a third party, and can deal with the property, while an excluded non-entitled spouse's consent has to be sought to a dealing by the resident entitled spouse, although in the event of a refusal to consent the court would in most cases readily dispense with consent.[4]

3–04. Application for an order

An application to the court for an exclusion order may be made by the entitled spouse, the non-entitled spouse or by either spouse where the spouses share the title to the home.[5] Even where the ground on which exclusion is sought is violence against a child of the family, the application must be made by a spouse. Rules of Court require an application to be intimated to the landlord where the matrimonial home is rented, and where the home is occupied by permission of a third party, to that third party.[6]

[1] 1983 S.L.T. 224.
[2] 1983 S.L.T. 275.
[3] See para. 1-07 for further details.
[4] See para. 6-10 below.
[5] s.4(1). S.4(7) provides that where both spouses share the title neither can exclude the other by means of an action of ejection. This overrules a dictum to the contrary in *Price* v. *Watson,* 1951 S.C. 359, *per* Lord President Cooper at p. 363.
[6] Rule of Court 188D(7) (Court of Session); Act of Sederunt (Applications under the Matrimonial Homes (Family Protection) (Scotland) Act 1981) 1982, rule 3 (Sheriff Court).

3-05. Where one spouse shares the right to occupy the home with a third party (*i.e.* a person other than his or her spouse), the other spouse has no occupancy rights unless that third party has waived (either expressly or by implication) his or her right to occupy the home.[7] In this situation the spouse without occupancy rights is not entitled to apply to the court for an order excluding either the other spouse or the third party. Furthermore, he or she may be ejected from the matrimonial home without the need for an exclusion order.

3-06. Dealing with the application

Sections 4(2) and (3) of the Act lay down a two-stage process for the consideration of an application for an exclusion order. First, under subsection (2) it must appear to the court that:

> "the making of the order is necessary for the protection of the applicant or any child of the family from any conduct or threatened or reasonably apprehended conduct of the non-applicant spouse which is or would be injurious to the physical or mental health of the applicant or child."

Secondly, if the court has decided that an order is necessary, subsection (3) directs it not to make such an order if it would be unjust or unreasonable having regard to various factors.[8] These two steps are discussed in the above order.

3-07. All the reported cases have been concerned with interim exclusion orders rather than with exclusion orders. It has been held, however, that the same tests are to be applied in deciding whether or not to grant an interim exclusion order as would apply to an application for an exclusion order.[9] The crucial phrase is "necessary for the protection of the applicant" which clearly means something more than the balance of convenience.[10]

3-08. *Absence from the home.* In *Bell* v. *Bell* Lords Robertson and Grieve opined that the test of necessity was unlikely to be satisfied where the applicant was not living in the home at the time of making the application.[11] By removing from the home the applicant removes the need for the other spouse to be excluded. This simplistic approach presents a victim of domestic violence with an unenviable choice; to stay in the home in the hope of success in an application for exclusion, or to leave the home and forgo any chance of returning. On the other hand the Lord Justice-Clerk (Lord Wheatley) was of the opinion that the applicant's absence from the home was a factor that the court should take into account, but that each case would depend on the reasons for such absence.[12] The latter view has prevailed, the Lord Justice-Clerk observing in *Colagiacomo* v. *Colagiacomo*:[13] "If there is any misconception that following *Bell* v. *Bell* an interim exclusion order will only be granted if the parties are both occupying the matrimonial home, the

---

[7] s.1(2). See para. 2-12 above.
[8] See para. 3-18 below.
[9] *Bell* v. *Bell*, 1983 S.L.T. 224, *per* Lord Justice-Clerk Wheatley at p. 227.
[10] *Smith* v. *Smith*, 1983 S.L.T. 275.
[11] 1983 S.L.T. 224 at pp. 230 and 233 respectively.
[12] at p. 228.
[13] 1983 S.L.T. 559 at p. 562.

sooner that misconception is removed the better." In *Brown* v. *Brown*[14] the fact that a victim of repeated violence had left the matrimonial home to live in a refuge was regarded as a factor in favour of the other spouse's exclusion. As Lord Dunpark put it, it was "prima facie a demonstration of desperation."[15] On the other hand, in *Stewart* v. *Stewart*[16] an application for an interim exclusion order by a wife was refused where her husband had bought a flat for himself and was not seeking to return to the matrimonial home.

3–09. Section 13(5) of the Law Reform (Miscellaneous Provisions) (Scotland) Act 1985 has amended section 4(1). This now provides that an application for an exclusion order may be made whether or not the applicant is in occupation of the matrimonial home at the time of the application.

3–10. *Alternative of interdict.* Another aspect of the test of necessity is whether alternative methods of protecting the applicant (principally a matrimonial interdict with or without a power of arrest attached) have first been considered. In *Bell* the applicant, Mrs Bell, had been granted an interim interdict against molestation and later applied for an interim exclusion order. This interdict had not been breached, nor did she aver that it was likely to be breached. In these circumstances it was held that an interim exclusion order was unnecessary, since she appeared to be protected by the interim interdict. Lord Grieve[17] remarked that: "In view of the provisions contained in ss. 14 to 17 [matrimonial interdicts] I am inclined to think that the remedy of a matrimonial interdict should be sought before that of an interim exclusion order." Lord Robertson[18] agreed. An interim exclusion order, "should in my opinion be regarded as an ultimate remedy in circumstances where interdict or a matrimonial interdict under s. 14 of the Act is inadequate." This approach could result in an applicant being subjected to further violence in order to demonstrate to the court that the interim interdict already granted did not give sufficient protection.

3–11. Later cases have adopted a slightly different approach. In *Ward* v. *Ward* an interim exclusion order was granted as the court thought it unlikely that, having regard to the defender's drink-related course of violent conduct, other means would secure the applicant's protection.[19] In *Colagiacomo* it was stressed that whether an interdict would provide the necessary protection would depend on the individual circumstances of the case; even if the couple were living apart an interim interdict might not suffice.[20] Finally in *Brown,* Lord Dunpark, delivering the opinion of the Second Division, stated that the remarks of Lords Robertson and Grieve in *Bell* must be seen in the context of that case.[21] The present position would seem to be that the judge must consider whether an alternative remedy would provide sufficient protection before granting an exclusion order, and, in coming to a view as to

14 1985 S.L.T. 376.
15 at p. 378.
16 Outer House, 1 June 1983 (unreported).
17 1983 S.L.T. 224 at p. 233.
18 at p. 231.
19 1983 S.L.T. 472 at p. 475.
20 1983 S.L.T. 559 at p. 562.
21 1985 S.L.T. 376 at p. 378.

the sufficiency of the alternatives, should have regard to all the circumstances of the case. It is not, however, true to say that an exclusion order may only be granted if an interdict has first been tried and shown to be insufficient.

3–12. Another aspect of the relationship between matrimonial interdicts and exclusion orders is the possibility of using the former to achieve exclusion. In *Tattersall* v. *Tattersall*[22] it was held that an interdict prohibiting entry and occupation of the home could not competently be granted against an entitled husband so as to eject him. An interdict is to prevent a wrong; it follows that it cannot, by itself, take away legal rights. It is therefore not possible by interdict alone[23] to deny an entitled spouse the right to remain in occupation of the matrimonial home. By parity of reasoning it would be incompetent to interdict the return of an entitled spouse who had been shut out of the home by the other spouse and who wished to re-occupy it.

3–13. Two other permutations are possible: the granting of an interdict prohibiting a resident non-entitled spouse from continuing to occupy the home, so that the non-resident entitled spouse can enter into and occupy the home alone; and the granting of a similar interdict to a resident entitled spouse in order to keep out the non-resident non-entitled spouse. The first permutation was expressly left open in *Brown*.[24] In principle, however, such an interdict should be incompetent.[25] A non-entitled spouse has, by virtue of section 1(1)(*a*) of the Act, a statutory right to continue to occupy the home, so that an interdict prohibiting this takes away an undoubted legal right just as an interdict prohibiting occupancy by virtue of title as owner or tenant does.

3–14. The second permutation raises slightly different issues. A non-entitled spouse who is not in occupation has, it is true, a statutory right under section 1(1)(*b*) to enter into and occupy the matrimonial home. But if entry is denied by the entitled spouse, leave of the court must be sought by the non-entitled spouse before the right can be exercised.[26] In deciding whether or not to grant leave, the court is to consider what would be just and reasonable having regard to various factors including the spouses' respective needs and resources and their conduct.[27] The test is clearly different from the need for protection from injurious conduct which forms the basis of an exclusion order. If the court came to the conclusion that it would be neither just nor reasonable to allow the non-entitled spouse to re-enter the home, that spouse's occupancy rights are effectively suspended by order of a court. An interdict against re-entry could then, it is submitted, be competently granted without infringing legal rights. A suggestion was made in *Tattersall* to this effect,[28] although the remarks were *obiter*.

---

[22] 1983 S.L.T. 506.
[23] An interdict may be granted once a spouse has been excluded. See s. 4(4)(*b*) and para. 3-30 below.
[24] 1985 S.L.T. 376 at p. 379.
[25] It is said to be standard practice in Glasgow Sheriff Court: P. Robson "Exclusion Orders under the Matrimonial Homes Act in 1985" (1985) 30 J.L.S. 299 at p. 301.
[26] s.1(3).
[27] s.3(3).
[28] 1983 S.L.T. 506 at p. 509.

3–15. On a commonsense level there is much to be said for the view that the only method of suspending a spouse's occupancy rights should be by means of an exclusion order, except where the non-entitled spouse has left the home and seeks leave of the court to re-enter. Even in this latter case leave ought to be refused only if the non-entitled spouse would have been excluded in an application by the entitled spouse for an exclusion order.[29] To set a lower standard for refusing leave to enter encourages entitled spouses to take the law into their own hands by throwing their non-entitled spouses out of the home, thus continuing one of the mischiefs which the Act was designed to stop. The different criteria for granting leave to enter and exclusion negatives such an approach.

3–16. *Seriousness of injury.* The seriousness of the injury or threatened injury to the applicant's physical or mental health is another factor which requires to be taken into account in deciding whether exclusion is necessary. In *Bell* v. *Bell,* one of the first cases to be decided, Lord Robertson expressed the view that the applicant must be in "real and immediate danger of serious injury or irreparable damage" to succeed,[30] and Lord Grieve in the same case used a similar phrase.[31] This test, which appears to derive from a Practice Note by the President of the Family Division of the High Court of England and Wales in connection with *ex parte* injunctions, has not been adopted in subsequent cases and must now be regarded as too severe. Clearly something more than the rows and disputes common amongst couples whose relationships are breaking up is looked for.[31a] An isolated physical assault out of character may not be sufficient to justify exclusion,[32] but violent behaviour coupled with evidence of frequent drunkenness will normally lead to exclusion.[33] It is not necessary that the applicant should have been physically assaulted: persistent harassment, threats or denigration which affect his or her mental health will suffice.[34]

3–17. Injury to children

An exclusion order may be made if it appears necessary for the protection of any child of the family.[35] Child of the family includes a child or grandchild of either spouse, and any person who has been brought up or accepted by either spouse as if he or she were a child of that spouse.[36] Although there is no age limit for a child of the family, a person is not likely to be excluded because of violence to adult children unless they live at home because of physical or mental disability. There is no requirement that the child whose protection is sought is living in the matrimonial home at the time of the application. For

[29] *Nimmo* v. *Nimmo,* Glasgow Sheriff Court, 12 Aug. 1983 (reported in (1984) 29 J.L.S. 4).

[30] 1983 S.L.T. 224 at p. 231.

[31] at p. 233.

[31a] *Matheson* v. *Matheson,* 1986 S.L.T. (Sh. Ct.) 2.

[32] *Gillespie* v. *Gillespie,* First Division, 11 May 1984 (unreported, but referred to at length in P. Robson, "Exclusion Orders under the Matrimonial Homes Act in 1985" (1985) 30 J.L.S. 299), where the sheriff's judgment in refusing an exclusion order was commended by the Inner House as being careful and sensitive.

[33] See, *e.g. Ward* v. *Ward,* 1983 S.L.T. 472.

[34] *McCafferty* v. *McCafferty,* Outer House, 7 Dec. 1984 (unreported).

[35] s.4(2). The application must be made by one of the spouses.

[36] s.22.

example, the child might be in care or staying with relatives, but would be able to return home if the violent spouse were excluded.

3–18. Whether exclusion would be unjustified or unreasonable

The second stage of the process of dealing with an application for an exclusion order is contained in section 4(3). This directs the court not to make an exclusion order if to do so would be unjustified or unreasonable. In considering whether it would be unjustified or unreasonable the court must have regard to all the circumstances of the case and in particular to the conduct of the spouses, their needs and resources, the needs of any child of the family, any business use of the home, and whether the entitled spouse has offered the non-entitled spouse suitable alternative accommodation.[37] One of the most important factors will be the availability of suitable alternative accommodation for both spouses and any children. The availability of temporary accommodation to the non-resident spouse from friends, relatives, refuges or the local authority is not usually sufficient to make it unjust and unreasonable to make an exclusion order. The special circumstances of the home may make exclusion inappropriate. For example, the home may have been specially adapted to meet the needs of a disabled spouse whose exclusion is sought. The resources of the spouses are also relevant, for it could be considered unjustified and unreasonable to exclude a spouse who was not able to afford alternative accommodation, while the applicant spouse had enough money to purchase another home.

3–19. Where children are involved it is generally regarded as being in their best interests to remain in, or go back to, the home together with the parent looking after them. Consideration of the children's welfare is, however, a factor in deciding whether exclusion would be unjust and unreasonable; it is not something that should be taken into account in deciding whether exclusion is necessary for the applicant spouse's protection. Thus it would be inappropriate to exclude a man from the matrimonial home where he and his wife could not live together, simply because his wife and children have a better claim to occupy the matrimonial home.[37a]

3–20. Business use of the home is another factor to be considered. Doctors and dentists often have their surgeries in part of their homes and could not readily carry on their profession if excluded from them. It is not clear whether it would be competent to exclude a person from the residential part of the home but allow him or her use of the surgery. The answer might depend on the extent to which the residence and business premises were capable of separate use.

3–21. Section 4(3)(*b*) deals with special kinds of matrimonial homes, farm-houses, and premises occupied under service tenancies or service occupancy agreements, where the spouse sought to be excluded is (or both spouses are) obliged to reside on the premises. Excluding a farm manager, a farm worker or a caretaker, for example, may result in the landlord or employer terminating the excluded spouse's right to occupy, so that the home ceases to be available to either spouse. However, if the spouse sought

[37] s.4(3)(*a*).
[37a] *Matheson* v. *Matheson,* 1986 S.L.T. (Sh. Ct.) 2.

to be excluded could find alternative accommodation locally which would enable him or her to continue to carry out the duties satisfactorily, an exclusion order might still be made. In these cases it would be helpful if evidence of the landlord's or employer's likely reaction was available to the court.

3–22. Post-divorce exclusion orders

Section 14(2)(*d*) of the Family Law (Scotland) Act 1985 empowers the court hearing an action of divorce[38] to make, on or after the granting of the decree,[39] an order excluding either spouse from the occupation of the former matrimonial home. Such an order could be useful in allowing one party to the marriage sole occupation of the former matrimonial home owned or tenanted solely by, or in common with, the other party.

3–23.   No criteria are set out in the 1985 Act for the granting of such orders. The fact that divorce ends the couple's marital relationship suggests that the criteria for exclusion orders contained in section 4 of the Matrimonial Homes Act relating to subsisting marriages would not be applicable.

3–24. Interim exclusion orders

While an application for an exclusion order is pending, the court is empowered under section 4(6) to order the other spouse to be excluded from the matrimonial home. This subsection contains no guidelines as to the circumstances in which an interim order should be granted. It might be thought that the court has an unfettered discretion, especially since subsection (6) expressly applies subsections (4) and (5), but omits any reference to subsections (2) and (3) which contain the guidelines for the making of exclusion orders. It has been decided[40] that the context of section 4(6) requires that the guidelines applying to exclusion orders apply equally to interim exclusion orders.

3–25.   In terms of the proviso to section 4(6) an interim exclusion order may be made only if the non-applicant spouse has been afforded an opportunity of being heard by, or represented before, the court. Rule 188D(9) of the Rules of the Court of Session requires seven days' notice of an application made by way of motion in a consistorial action but the court may, on cause shown, set a lesser period. A seven day or lesser period would also apply to an application made in another fashion—in the original summons for example. In the sheriff court most applications under the Act are dealt with as ordinary causes[41] where the period is 14 days unless shortened by the sheriff. But applications for interim orders are heard as soon as convenient. In *Brown* v. *Brown*[42] an interim exclusion order was made two days after service of the initial writ containing the application on the defender. The Court of Session rule seems preferable, as two days must in

---

[38] or nullity: 1985 Act, s. 17.
[39] 1985 Act, s.14(3).
[40] *Bell* v. *Bell*, 1983 S.L.T. 224; *Smith* v. *Smith*, 1983 S.L.T. 275; *Ward* v. *Ward*, 1983 S.L.T. 472.
[41] Act of Sederunt (Applications under the Matrimonial Homes (Family Protection) (Scotland) Act 1981) 1982, rule 5.
[42] 1985 S.L.T. 376.

many cases give defenders and their solicitors insufficient time to prepare their case.

3–26. While an application for an interim exclusion order is pending, the applicant may apply for an interim interdict prohibiting further violence or molestation. Such an interdict may be granted immediately and be served on the other spouse together with the application for an interim exclusion order. The danger of this course of action is that it becomes open to the defender to argue against the granting of the interim exclusion order on the basis that the interim interdict is being obtempered and exclusion is therefore not necessary.[43] Against this has to be set the possibility of renewed violence following service of the application for exclusion and the need for protection by way of interdict.

3–27. Evidence in support of applications
In the case of an application for an exclusion order a full proof will be necessary if the application is defended. Where applications for interim exclusion orders are concerned, something less than a full proof but more than *ex parte* averments and answers is required. The court has to have something before it which supports the applicant's case. The types of evidence that might be adduced at the interim stage include extracts of previous convictions for assault or breach of the peace, doctors' certificates as to the applicant's health,[44] an investigation and report on the children's circumstances,[45] and affidavits from relatives or neighbours.[46] Another possible course of action is for the judge to interview the two parties privately.[47]

3–28. Evidence submitted in the form of affidavits is admissible in the Court of Session in connection with any application under the Act.[48] In the sheriff court the use of affidavits is limited to opposed applications for interim orders.[49] In the absence of wider statutory sanction affidavit evidence is otherwise inadmissible.

3–29. Ancillary orders
An exclusion order or an interim exclusion order by itself only suspends the right of the excluded spouse to occupy the matrimonial home. In order to make an (interim) exclusion order effective and to deal with consequential matters, subsections (4) and (5) of section 4 confer power on the court to make various ancillary orders. These fall into three groups.

3–30. First, the court must, if requested to do so, grant an interdict prohibiting the excluded spouse from entering the matrimonial home without the express permission of the other spouse.[50] If the excluded spouse wishes to see the children or uplift personal effects, it would be better to seek permission

[43] *Bell* v. *Bell,* 1983 S.L.T. 224.
[44] *Colagiacomo* v. *Colagiacomo,* 1983 S.L.T. 559.
[45] *Ward* v. *Ward,* 1983 S.L.T. 472.
[46] *Brown* v. *Brown,* 1985 S.L.T. 376.
[47] *Gillespie* v. *Gillespie,* First Division, 11 May 1984 (unreported).
[48] Rule of Court 188D(15).
[49] Act of Sederunt (Consistorial Causes) 1984, para. 3 (15).
[50] s.4(4)(*b*).

beforehand rather than risk a scene and possible breach of interdict by arriving unannounced.

3–31. Secondly, the court must grant a warrant for the summary ejection of the excluded spouse from the matrimonial home,[51] and an interdict prohibiting him or her from removing any of the furniture and plenishings[52] (whether or not they are subject to a use and possession order)[53] except with the written consent of the other spouse or the leave of the court, unless the excluded spouse satisfies the court that they are unnecessary.[54] For example, the excluded spouse may have left the home voluntarily and be prepared to give an undertaking not to remove items from the home.

3–32. Thirdly, the court has a discretion whether to grant the orders set out in section 4(5). The only one of these that calls for comment is the interdict prohibiting the excluded spouse from being in a specified area in the vicinity of the matrimonial home.[55] The purpose of this interdict is to prevent the excluded spouse intimidating the other by loitering on the stair or in the street outside the matrimonial home. An unsuccessful attempt was made during the passage of the Law Reform (Miscellaneous Provisions) (Scotland) Act 1985 to extend the scope of such interdicts so as to prohibit the excluded spouse from the other spouse's place of work, or the children's school, or specified areas in the vicinity of these places. Molestation at places outwith the immediate vicinity of the matrimonial home can be prohibited by a matrimonial interdict to which a power of arrest is attachable.[56]

3–33. Where the court excludes an ex-spouse from the occupation of the former matrimonial home after divorce,[57] it is empowered to grant any ancillary order which is expedient to give effect to the exclusion order.[58] The types of ancillary orders set out in section 4(4) and (5) of the Act would also be appropriate in the case of post-divorce exclusion.

3–34. Recall and termination

An exclusion order, an interim exclusion order or any of the ancillary orders may, on application, be varied or recalled by the court.[59] Apart from this an exclusion order (or an interim exclusion order) terminates automatically, together with the ancillary orders, on the termination of the marriage due to death, divorce or annulment.[60] They also terminate when the entitled spouse (whether or not the excluded spouse) ceases to be entitled or permitted to occupy the home,[61] or, in the case of jointly entitled spouses, when both spouses cease to be so entitled or permitted.[62]

---

[51] s.4(4)(*a*).
[52] s.4(4)(*c*).
[53] Under s.3(2).
[54] s.4(4).
[55] s.4(5)(*a*).
[56] See Chap. 5.
[57] Under the Family Law (Scotland) Act 1985, s.14(2)(*d*); see para. 3-22 above.
[58] 1985 Act, s.14(2)(*k*).
[59] s.5(1).
[60] s.5(1)(*a*). The court can make a fresh exclusion order on or after granting a decree of divorce or nullity; see para. 3-22 above.
[61] Subject to s.6(1): s.5(1)(*b*) and see para. 2-54 above.
[62] s.5(1)(*c*).

3-35. Exclusion and homelessness

Exclusion and homelessness are connected in at least three ways. First, an exclusion order forces the excluded spouse to find alternative accommodation. Secondly, while an application for exclusion is pending many applicants seek temporary refuge away from the matrimonial home. Thirdly, victims of domestic violence can avoid the difficulties and uncertainties of obtaining an exclusion order by getting permanent accommodation for themselves elsewhere. A local authority is, under the Housing (Homeless Persons) Act 1977, obliged to secure that accommodation becomes available to applicants who fulfil certain conditions, including being homeless, not being intentionally homeless and being in priority need.[63]

3-36. Excluded spouses while not intentionally homeless are rarely in priority need. They are therefore unlikely to obtain permanent local authority accommodation, particularly as there is a shortage of houses for single people. The lack of accommodation is a factor which the court would have regard to in deciding whether it would be unjust or unreasonable to grant an exclusion order.[64]

3-37. Victims of domestic violence who have found accommodation in refuges or similar places should, according to the Code of Guidance on the Housing (Homeless Persons) Act issued by the Scottish Development Department, still be regarded as homeless since such accommodation is not intended to be permanent.[65] The code also offers the view that victims who leave home rather than endure further violence should not be treated as intentionally homeless.[66] Given that interdicts cannot offer complete protection, especially where the violence is linked to drink, and that exclusion orders are difficult to obtain, the code's approach seems sensible. Most victims of domestic violence will be in priority need because they have dependent children.[67] Victims without children should, the code suggests,[68] be treated as being in priority need due to their vulnerability,[69] but this interpretation is not widely followed in practice.

[63] 1977 Act, s.4(5). See para. 7-11 below.
[64] See para. 3-18 above.
[65] Para. 4.14.
[66] Para. 2.17, but see para. 7-11 below.
[67] 1977 Act, s. 2(1)(a).
[68] Para. 2.13c.
[69] 1977 Act, s.2 (1)(c) "other special reason."

CHAPTER 4

TRANSFER OF TENANCY ORDERS

4–01. Introduction

Before the Tenants' Rights, Etc. (Scotland) Act 1980 public sector tenants, unlike most private sector tenants, had no security of tenure. Local authority landlords were able to effect transfers of tenancies from one spouse to another as a matter of administrative discretion. Once security of tenure was conferred, some kind of judicial process became necessary in order to effect transfers in the public sector. As a holding measure until the enactment and coming into force of the Matrimonial Homes Act, the 1980 Act enabled a public sector landlord to apply to the court for recovery of possession on the ground that the landlord wished to transfer the tenancy to the spouse or former spouse of the tenant on marital breakdown.[1] This provision was repealed and replaced by section 13 of the Matrimonial Homes Act which empowers the court to transfer the tenancy of a matrimonial home (public or private sector) from the tenant to his or her spouse, either during marriage or on divorce or annulment.

4–02. Application for an order

An application for a tenancy transfer order may be made by the spouse[2] of the tenant. Where both spouses share the tenancy, either can apply for an order vesting the tenancy solely in the applicant.[3] It is not possible for one co-tenant's share of a tenancy to be transferred to his or her spouse where the other co-tenant is a third party. An application is capable of being made by a spouse who has renounced occupancy rights, because he or she remains a non-entitled spouse. While the courts would be unlikely to grant a transfer against the wishes of the tenant in favour of a spouse who had renounced, they might do so where the transfer application was rendered necessary by the landlord's refusal to consent to an assignation by the tenant. The right to apply for a tenancy transfer order could be renounced either in the same document as a renunciation of occupancy rights or separately.[4]

4–03. The subject of a transfer application has to be the tenancy of a matrimonial home. Tenancy includes a statutory tenancy and a subtenancy.[5] The court has no power under the Act to transfer the tenancy of a matrimonial home which is let on a long lease or in connection with employment, or is (or is part of) an agricultural holding, a croft, the land of a tenant-at-will or a similar holding.[6] However, such excluded tenancies are transferable by the court on divorce or annulment under the Family Law

---

[1] Para. 6 of Pt. I of Sched. 2. See para. 4-14 below.
[2] s.13(1). See Chap. 7 for the position of cohabitees.
[3] s.13(9).
[4] s.16(1) of the Family Law (Scotland) Act 1985 empowers the court to set aside or vary an agreement as to financial provision to be made on divorce. This could be used to set aside a renunciation of the right to apply for a tenancy transfer order on divorce.
[5] s.22.
[6] s.13(7).

(Scotland) Act 1985.[7] Where the matrimonial home forms a part of the subjects of the lease (the manager's flat in a hotel, for example) a transfer of the home only would replace one tenant by two and render many of the provisions of the lease inapt. This suggests that transfer is only competent where the matrimonial home forms the entire subjects of a lease.[8]

4–04. An application for a tenancy transfer order has to be made during marriage. An application afterwards is too late, since the court is directed to exercise its powers either during marriage or on granting a decree of divorce or nullity.[9] Where the court refuses a divorce or annulment it can still grant a tenancy transfer order, because the applicant remains a non-entitled spouse. The Act makes no provision for the granting of an interim transfer pending the determination of an application for a tenancy transfer order.

4–05. Position of the landlord

The landlord must be notified of an application for a transfer of the tenancy and is entitled to be heard.[10] Notification is done by the non-entitled spouse serving a copy of the application on the landlord. Landlords may wish to comment on the applicant's suitability to become the tenant and his or her ability to pay the rent and perform any other obligations contained in the lease. It appears from the Institute of Housing/Scottish Homeless Group Report that public sector landlords do not generally object.[11] Where objections are made it is usually on the ground that there are arrears of rent which the landlord is trying to recover from the tenant. However, a local authority landlord might also object where the result of a transfer would be to give the tenancy of a family-sized home to the spouse not looking after the children. The report urges local authorities actively to support a transfer application made on marital breakdown by the spouse with greatest housing need (usually a wife with the children).[12]

4–06. Factors taken into account

In deciding whether to grant a tenancy transfer order the court is directed to have regard to all the circumstances of the case including the conduct of the spouses, their needs and resources, the needs of any child of the family, any business use of the house, and whether the tenant (or co-tenant) spouse has offered the applicant suitable alternative accommodation.[13] Also relevant are the suitability and financial capacity of the applicant to become the tenant.[14] In *Sleboda* v. *Sleboda*[15] a transfer on divorce was refused on the basis that the tenant husband would be deprived of a home for himself and his son whereas the wife had already obtained suitable rent-free accommodation elsewhere. But in *McGowan* v. *McGowan*[16] an order was granted as the tenant husband's adultery and other intolerable behaviour caused the

---

[7] 1985 Act, ss. 8(1)(*a*) and 27(1).
[8] Matrimonial home may may include other ground or buildings; see s.22 and para. 2-14 above.
[9] s.13(1) and (2).
[10] s.13(4).
[11] Para. 4.7. See para. 1-07 above.
[12] Para. 4.8.
[13] s.13(3) applying s.3(3)(*a*)-(*e*).
[14] s.13(3). The availability of housing benefit may affect financial capacity.
[15] Outer House, 4 Feb. 1983 (unreported but noted in (1983) 28 J.L.S. 420).
[16] 1986 S.L.T. 112.

marriage to break down and the wife and son were having to share a small flat with her married daughter and family.

4–07. Effect of a tenancy transfer order

A tenancy transfer order vests the tenancy in the applicant spouse directly.[17] Unlike ordinary assignations, intimation to the landlord is not necessary for the completion of the new tenant's title. The clerk of the court granting the order is under a duty to notify the landlord of the making of the order.[18] All the rights and obligations under the lease are taken over by the new tenant, except arrears of rent due at the date of transfer.[19] These remain the responsibility of the former tenant, or, in the case of co-tenant spouses, the joint and several responsibility of the co-tenants.[20] The obligations taken over include not only obligations arising after transfer, such as paying rent in future and keeping the garden tidy, but also prior obligations which the former tenant left unfulfilled. For example, if the former tenant had failed to pay for damage caused to the home before the transfer for which he or she was liable under the lease, the cost would be recoverable from the new tenant.

4–08. As mentioned in the previous paragraph the former tenant remains liable for any arrears of rent. Once the tenancy transfer order has been granted the landlord can no longer bring, or threaten to bring, proceedings for recovery of possession of the home as long as the new tenant pays future rent timeously. The landlord's remedy is a payment action for the arrears brought against the former tenant. Since this may be ineffective, the landlord may object to the tenancy transfer application and/or bring proceedings for recovery of possession in order to put pressure on the tenant to come to an arrangement for the payment of the arrears.

4–09. A tenancy transfer order has little effect upon the rights of either spouse during their marriage to occupy the home, because the home does not cease to be a matrimonial home. The applicant, on becoming the tenant, becomes the entitled spouse and acquires occupancy rights by virtue of title in place of his or her statutory occupancy rights as spouse of the former tenant. Conversely, the former tenant loses his or her occupancy rights by virtue of title, but acquires instead the statutory occupancy rights conferred on a non-entitled spouse.

4–10. The position is very different where the tenancy is transferred on divorce or annulment. This is because of the absence of statutory occupancy rights after dissolution of marriage.[21] If no order were to be made the tenant would be entitled to sole occupation of the former matrimonial home; a tenancy transfer order transfers this entitlement to the other party to the marriage.

---

[17] s.13(5).
[18] s.13(6).
[19] s.13(5).
[20] s.13(10)(c).
[21] Although the court has power to grant occupancy rights after divorce (Family Law (Scotland) Act 1985, s.14(2)(d)), it is inconceivable that the court would grant occupancy to the former tenant while transferring the tenancy to his or her ex-spouse.

4–11. A statutory tenancy may be inherited by the surviving spouse or another member of the family on the tenant's death. Another succession is allowed on the death of the first successor, but no further inheritance is permitted.[22] A secure tenancy in the public sector may be inherited likewise, but on the death of the original tenant only.[23] A tenancy transfer order has no effect on these rules beyond substituting the transferee for the former tenant. Thus if there had already been two successions before the order was granted, a statutory tenancy comes to an end on the death of the transferee.

4–12. Compensation

The court, on granting a tenancy transfer order, has power to order the new tenant to pay compensation to the former tenant.[24] The amount of compensation is what seems to the court to be just and reasonable in all the circumstances of the case. Relevant factors would include the amount of the former tenant's loss and the financial circumstances of the spouses. Because a transfer between spouses does not significantly affect their rights to occupy, questions of compensation are only likely to arise where the tenancy has a market value or is transferred on dissolution of marriage. Where a transfer is made on divorce or annulment, the financial provision[25] may be adjusted to reflect the former tenant's loss of entitlement to occupy and any removal costs. Compensation is not payable for the loss of the former tenant's right, under the Tenants' Rights, Etc. (Scotland) Act 1980, to purchase at a discount the house of which he or she was the secure tenant.[26] Consideration of the financial circumstances of the spouses will also limit awards, since many people living in rented accommodation cannot afford much in the way of compensation.

4–13. Alternatives to tenancy transfer orders

It would appear from the Institute of Housing/Scottish Homeless Group Report[27] that not many applications are made for tenancy transfer orders.[28] This is perhaps not so surprising, since as long as the couple remain married an order makes little or no difference to their occupancy rights. The new tenant has, however, the satisfaction of having the house in his or her own name and is safe from an action of recovery of possession on the basis of the former tenant's arrears of rent. Furthermore, there are other ways of transferring tenancies. First, the tenant's spouse may take over the tenancy without going to court as long as both the tenant and the landlord consent.[29] This administrative procedure is simpler and cheaper than proceedings under section 13 of the Act. Secondly, the landlord may recover possession by court proceedings against the tenant and then grant a new tenancy to the former tenant's spouse. Although court proceedings are involved, the

---

[22] Rent (Scotland) Act 1984, s.3 and Sched. 1.
[23] Tenants' Rights, Etc. (Scotland) Act 1980, s.13.
[24] s.13(1) and (9).
[25] The Family Law (Scotland) Act 1985, s.17 empowers the court to award financial provision on granting decree of nullity.
[26] s.13(11).
[27] See para. 1-07 above.
[28] Para. 4.1. In the first 14-15 months of the Act 172 applications were made relating to the 38 housing authorities (rather more than half the total number in Scotland) responding to the question.
[29] A secure tenancy may be assigned with the consent of the landlord, which consent is not to be unreasonably withheld. Tenants' Rights, Etc. (Scotland) Act 1980, s.21 and Sched. 3.

pursuer is the landlord rather than the prospective new tenant. Another possible advantage of repossession followed by reletting is that the home may not be a matrimonial home afterwards as long as the former tenant does not live in it after the reletting. It could be argued that recovery of possession, by terminating the tenancy, terminates the existence of the previous matrimonial home, and that the relet home is not a new matrimonial home since it is neither provided nor made available by the local authority or the new tenant as a residence for both spouses, nor has it become one.[30] On the other hand the courts may regard the home as continuing to be a matrimonial home but with a change of tenant.

4–14. The above report[31] found that a large majority of the local authorities surveyed favoured a return to the pre-Act position whereby a local authority landlord, at the request of the non-tenant spouse, could apply to the court for recovery of possession on the ground that the spouse or former spouse of the tenant no longer wished to live with the tenant and the local authority wished to transfer the secure tenancy to the spouse or former spouse.[32] Changes may be made within the next year or so, since the Government is understood[33] to be considering whether to implement a recommendation along the above lines contained in the report.[34]

[30] s.22. See paras. 2-16 to 2-17 above.
[31] Para. 4.15.
[32] Reinstating para. 6 of Pt. I of Sched. 2 to the Tenants' Rights, Etc. (Scotland) Act 1980 which was repealed by s.13 of the Matrimonial Homes Act.
[33] (1985) 108 SCOLAG Bul. 143.
[34] Para. 4.22.

CHAPTER 5

MATRIMONIAL INTERDICTS AND POWERS OF ARREST

5–01. Matrimonial interdicts

The Act introduced a new species of interdict termed a matrimonial interdict. Notwithstanding the use of the term matrimonial interdict, such an interdict can be granted on the application of a cohabiting partner in certain circumstances.[1] The special feature of matrimonial interdicts is the possibility of attaching a power of arrest to them, thus involving the police in their enforcement. Although giving the police a role in the enforcement of orders of the civil courts is unusual,[2] the advantage of the police is that they are the only agency who are readily available at any hour of the day or night and who possess sufficient powers.

5–02. A matrimonial interdict is defined by section 14(2) as an interdict (including an interim interdict) which prohibits any conduct by one spouse towards the other or a child of the family,[3] or which prohibits entry to the matrimonial home or a specified area in the vicinity of the home. Examples include an interdict prohibiting physical violence by a husband against his wife or a wife annoying her husband by persistent telephoning at unreasonable times. On the other hand, interdicts prohibiting the removal of furniture and plenishings from a matrimonial home, interference with personal effects or disposal of the home in which a non-entitled cohabiting partner has occupancy rights, would seem not to fall into the category of matrimonial interdicts. Although the conduct prohibited would affect the other spouse it may not count as conduct towards him or her. The word "towards" indicates some restriction, for if it was intended that any conduct which affected a spouse could be prohibited by matrimonial interdict, section 14(2)(b) (interdict against spouse entering or remaining in matrimonial home to be a matrimonial interdict) would be superfluous.

5–03. Like other interdicts, a matrimonial interdict is competent only to prevent a threatened legal wrong; it cannot of itself take away a person's legal rights. In *Tattersall* v. *Tattersall* the Lord Ordinary excluded an entitled husband from the matrimonial home by means of an interdict under section 14(2)(b) which prohibited him from entering or remaining in the home. On a successful reclaiming motion the Inner House[4] held such an interdict to be incompetent, since neither expressly nor by implication did the Act provide for exclusion by this means. To permit exclusion from the matrimonial home simply by means of a matrimonial interdict would circumvent the stringent tests which have to be satisfied before an exclusion order can be granted.[5] The main purpose of section 14(2)(b) is to provide that

---

[1] See Chap. 7.
[2] *Caldwell* v. *Caldwell,* 1983 S.L.T. 610.
[3] See para. 2-07, above.
[4] 1983 S.L.T. 506.
[5] See s.4(2) and (3).

where the court has granted an exclusion order under section 4(2) (or an interim exclusion order under section 4(6)), the interdict or interdicts under section 4(4)(*a*) (prohibiting entry to the home) or 4(5)(*a*) (prohibiting entry to a specified area in the vicinity of the home) can have powers of arrest attached to them.

5–04. In *Tattersall* it was also suggested that a section 14(2)(*b*) interdict might be granted to prevent a non-entitled spouse refused entry to the matrimonial interdict ancillary to an exclusion order or an interim exclusion court decides that it would be neither just nor reasonable to grant the non-entitled spouse leave to enter.[6] This problem is discussed further in Chapter 3.[7]

5–05. Powers of arrest

The court is required, on application, to attach a power of arrest to any matrimonial interdict ancillary to an exclusion order or an interim exclusion order.[8] Such interdicts include those prohibiting entry to the matrimonial home or a specified area in the vicinity. For other matrimonial interdicts the court must, on application, attach a power of arrest as long as the spouse to be interdicted has been notified that a power of arrest has been applied for and has been given the opportunity to oppose it, and provided the court considers that in all the circumstances a power of arrest is necessary.[9]

5–06. A power of arrest may be attached to an existing interdict, even one granted before the Act came into force, provided it falls within the definition of a matrimonial interdict. For example, an interim interdict against molestation may be granted without intimation to the other spouse. He or she must, however, be given an opportunity to oppose the subsequent attachment of a power of arrest. In the Court of Session seven days' notice at least of an application for attachment is required, but the court can on cause shown allow a lesser period.[10] In the sheriff court such an application proceeds as an ordinary cause,[11] the period of notice being 14 days unless shortened by the sheriff.

5–07. The power of arrest is not effective until the relative interdict has been served on the spouse,[12] even though the interdict is valid (*e.g.* an interdict granted in the presence of the spouse). The interdict itself must be served. If the interlocutor granting the interdict sets out the conduct prohibited, service of a copy of the interlocutor would suffice. But where the interlocutor merely grants interdict as craved in the initial writ or summons, a copy of that document would have to be served as well, so that the spouse knows precisely what conduct is prohibited. Any power of arrest ceases to be valid on termination of the marriage.[13] A power of arrest may be recalled leaving the relative interdict standing, but normally both the interdict and the power of arrest would be recalled together.

[6] Under s.3(3) or (4).
[7] Paras. 3-12 to 3-15 above.
[8] s.15(1)(*a*).
[9] s.15(1)(*b*).
[10] Rule of Court 188D(9).
[11] Act of Sederunt (Applications under the Matrimonial Homes (Family Protection) (Scotland) Act 1981) 1982, rule 5.
[12] s.15(2).
[13] s.15(2).

5–08. It is common practice for a matrimonial interdict to be obtained and a power of arrest to be attached later, perhaps after a breach has occurred. Section 15(2) does not impose a duty to intimate the later attachment to the interdicted spouse, although intimation has to be made to the police,[14] and the spouse will have had an opportunity to oppose attachment.[15] Nevertheless it is clearly sensible to intimate, since it impresses upon the interdicted spouse the more severe consequences of a future breach. Moreover, the fact that a power of arrest has not been intimated may tip the balance against arrest in a case where the police are weighing up in their minds whether to arrest. Rules of Court might with advantage be made requiring the applicant spouse's solicitor to intimate to the other spouse the attachment of a power of arrest.

5–09. Under the Act any interdict granted on or after divorce or annulment cannot have a power of arrest attached to it. Section 14(2)(*d*) of the Family Law (Scotland) Act 1985 empowers the court to make orders regulating the occupation of the former matrimonial home after divorce and excluding one of the former spouses from it. Although the court has the power to make any ancillary order expedient to give effect to such an exclusion order,[16] it is considered that this does not extend to attaching a power of arrest to any interdict, in the absence of express provisions to that effect.[17]

5–10. A power of arrest enables a police officer to arrest without warrant a spouse reasonably suspected of being in breach of the matrimonial interdict to which it is attached.[18] The officer has a discretion; like many other statutes[19] which confer a power of arrest without warrant, section 15(3) provides that "a constable may arrest". Instead of arresting the offending spouse by virtue of the power of arrest, the police officer may arrest him or her for an offence, such as assault.[20] The guidance presently given to the police emphasises that the presumption should be that the spouse would be arrested unless the breach is trivial or unintentional, or possibly where he or she has left the scene and there is no likelihood of violence.[21] During the passage of the Law Reform (Miscellaneous Provisions) (Scotland) Act 1985 several attempts were made to convert this power of arrest into a duty to arrest by substituting "shall" for "may" in section 15(3). It was argued that a duty to arrest would remove any difference in interpretation between the police and aggrieved spouses as to what constitutes a trivial breach, and would require the police in all cases to pursue an offender to effect an arrest. These attempts were unsuccessful, though the

---

[14] Para. 5-11.

[15] s.15(1)(*b*).

[16] Family Law (Scotland) Act 1985, s.14(2)(*k*).

[17] s.14(5) of the 1985 Act brings certain sections of the Matrimonial Homes Act (but not those relating to matrimonial interdicts) into force when the court makes an occupation order.

[18] s.15(3).

[19] Road Traffic Act 1972, s.100 (arrest of driver suspected of being disqualified); Child Abduction Act 1984, s.7 (arrest of person suspected of taking or sending child out of U.K.).

[20] See para. 5-13 below.

[21] H.C. Deb., 1st Standing Scottish Committee, 5 Feb. 1985, col. 227; H.L. Deb., Vol. 467. col. 188 (30 Jul. 1985).

Lord Advocate stated[22] that he is to consider whether some strengthening or clarification of the guidelines would be helpful.

5–11. Notification of powers of arrest to police

The duty to notify the police of the existence of a power of arrest falls on the spouse who obtained the interdict. A police officer called out cannot be expected to rely on the word of the aggrieved spouse that a power of arrest exists; its existence and the precise terms of the interdict must be capable of being ascertained from police records. Section 15(4) lays a duty on the applicant spouse to ensure that there is delivered to the chief constable of the police area[23] in which the matrimonial home is situated (and also the chief constable of the police area in which the applicant spouse resides, if different), a copy of the application for the interdict and of the interlocutor granting the interdict, together with a certificate of service of the interdict on the interdicted spouse. This duty is reiterated in the Rules of the Court of Session which also require the applicant spouse to ensure that there is lodged in process a certificate that delivery has been duly effected.[24] There is no equivalent rule for sheriff court interdicts. Although a power of arrest is not invalidated by a failure to notify it to the police, the police can hardly be expected to exercise their powers of arrest in such a case.

5–12. Notification is effected by delivering the documents to the chief constable (at the headquarters of the force) who then arranges for copies to be sent to the appropriate divisional police office and the police office nearest the matrimonial home. There is always a danger of a renewal of violence soon after the interdict has been served upon the spouse. Speed in notifying the police can therefore be vital. The most effective method is to instruct an officer of court to serve the interdict and to deliver the appropriate documents forthwith thereafter to the police. Alternatively the aggrieved spouse's solicitor could serve the interdict postally, and at the same time post or deliver the required documents to the police. Where there is a real danger of further violence, a copy of the documents should be sent directly to the local police office as well as to the chief constable.[25]

5–13. The procedures described in paragraphs 5-10 and 5-11 above are also required to be followed where the interdict is varied or recalled.[26] Where a power of arrest ceases on divorce or annulment, Rules of Court lay a duty on the pursuer spouse to deliver a copy of the interlocutor granting the divorce or annulment to the police and to lodge a certificate of delivery in the process.[27]

5–14. Procedure following arrest

The procedure following on an arrest under a power of arrest attached to a matrimonial interdict is contained in sections 16 and 17 of the Act and is set out in the following diagram and accompanying notes. Where the offending

---

[22] H.L. Deb., Vol. 467, col. 188 (30 Jul. 1985).
[23] Local Government (Scotland) Act 1973, s.146.
[24] Rule of Court 188D(12).
[25] Advice from Crown Agent: (1983) 28 J.L.S. 274.
[26] s.15(5).
[27] Rule of Court 188D(13) (Court of Session); Act of Sederunt (Applications under the Matrimonial Homes (Family Protection) (Scotland) Act 1981) 1982, rule 9 inserted by Act of Sederunt (Consistorial Causes) 1984, para. 4 (sheriff court).

spouse has been arrested for an offence, such as a breach of the peace or an assault, and it transpires at the police office that a matrimonial interdict with a power of arrest is in existence and was breached, the police re-arrest under the power of arrest. This keeps available to the procurator fiscal the option of charging the spouse with an offence or presenting a petition under section 17. If the statutory power of arrest is not exercised, sections 16 and 17 do not apply and the normal criminal procedure has to be followed.

5–15. The purpose of the further period of detention which can be ordered by the sheriff on petition by the procurator fiscal, is to give the aggrieved spouse a period free from the possibility of further molestation or assault in which to take proceedings for breach of interdict. The procurator fiscal's petition is presented to the sheriff sitting as a court of summary criminal jurisdiction for the district in which the offending spouse was arrested, but the proceedings for breach of interdict require to be brought in the court which granted the interdict.

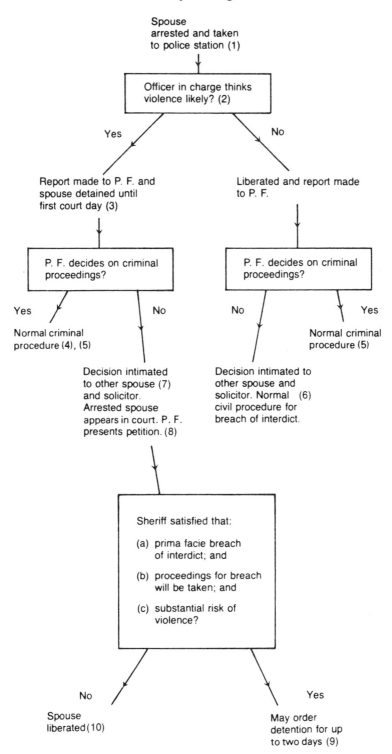

Spouse
arrested and taken
to police station (1)

Officer in charge thinks
violence likely? (2)

Yes

No

Report made to P. F. and
spouse detained until
first court day (3)

Liberated and report made
to P. F.

P. F. decides on criminal
proceedings?

P. F. decides on criminal
proceedings?

Yes

No

No

Yes

Normal criminal
procedure (4), (5)

Normal criminal
procedure (5)

Decision intimated
to other spouse (7)
and solicitor.
Arrested spouse
appears in court. P. F.
presents petition. (8)

Decision intimated to
other spouse and
solicitor. Normal   (6)
civil procedure for
breach of interdict.

Sheriff satisfied that:

(a) prima facie breach
of interdict; and

(b) proceedings for breach
will be taken; and

(c) substantial risk of
violence?

No

Yes

Spouse
liberated (10)

May order
detention for up
to two days (9)

Notes on diagram

(1) The arrested spouse has no express entitlement to have intimation of the arrest sent to a solicitor or to have a private interview before appearance in court,[28] but in practice this is permitted. The arrested spouse does have the right (subject to delay in the interests of justice) to have intimation of the arrest and place of custody sent to a named person.[29] The arrested spouse may be liable to be searched and fingerprinted.[30]

(2) The officer in charge of the police station may liberate the arrested spouse.[31] Provided the officer exercises the discretion to refuse to liberate in good faith, he or she is not subject to any claim for unlawful detention.

(3) The day on which the arrested spouse is to appear before the court is calculated by reference to section 17(2). A spouse arrested on Friday evening would appear on Tuesday if Monday was a court holiday and the court did not sit either on Saturday or Monday.

(4) Where the procurator fiscal decides to take criminal proceedings the normal practice would be for the offending spouse to remain in custody until the next court day.

(5) Breach of interdict proceedings may be brought after the conclusion of the criminal proceedings.

(6) Where the offence is minor but a breach of interdict has occurred, the procurator fiscal may decide to take no proceedings in respect of the offence, leaving it to the spouse to bring civil proceedings for breach of interdict.

(7) Once the procurator fiscal has decided not to take criminal proceedings, this fact must be intimated at the earliest opportunity to the aggrieved spouse and his or her solicitor. The police may be able to tell the procurator fiscal of the name and address of the solicitor if this appears on the interdict documents; alternatively they can ask the aggrieved spouse when making the arrest. Under section 17(2) of the Act the procurator fiscal "shall wherever practicable" bring the offending spouse before the sheriff. This suggests there is a discretion to release[32] where a petition will clearly be refused, for example when the aggrieved spouse's solicitor states that no breach of interdict proceedings are to be brought. Perhaps because section 17 petitions are not purely criminal proceedings, fiscals as a matter of practice present a petition in every case where they decide not to take criminal proceedings. By presenting a petition the Crown is deemed to have abandoned its right to initiate criminal proceedings at a later stage.

(8) The procurator fiscal's petition states the facts and circumstances of the incident giving rise to the breach of interdict and the arrest and craves the sheriff to grant warrant for the offending spouse to be detained for a further period not exceeding two days. In most cases the aggrieved spouse will be represented. Her (or his) solicitor could confirm that breach of interdict proceedings are to be brought, and put before the sheriff past incidents and

---

[28] s.305 of the Criminal Procedure (Scotland) Act 1975 applies only to proceedings under Pt. II of that Act.

[29] s.17(3) applying s.3(1) and (2) of the Criminal Justice (Scotland) Act 1980.

[30] Renton and Brown, *Criminal Procedure* (5th ed.), para. 5-30.

[31] s.16(1). Ss. 295 and 298 of the Criminal Procedure (Scotland) Act 1975 (interim liberation by police and bail) do not apply.

[32] Under s.321(3) of the Criminal Procedure (Scotland) Act 1975 the procurator fiscal "shall wherever practicable" bring an arrested person before the court. Nevertheless there is a discretion to order release.

other facts in support of the crave for further detention. The procurator fiscal's role will in these cases be limited. Where the aggrieved spouse is not represented, the procurator fiscal has to place all relevant facts before the court. The arrested spouse is entitled to the services of the duty solicitor, and will be given an opportunity to address the sheriff.

(9) The warrant for imprisonment now states the date and hour of release. Prison standing orders provide that the day of reception counts as the first day and the day of release (usually at 8 a.m.) as the second day. Imprisonment for a further two days often resulted in no more than overnight detention. In working out the time of release no account is taken of any Saturday, Sunday or court holiday of the court in which the breach of interdict proceedings are to be brought, in order to give the aggrieved spouse two clear working days in which to bring breach of interdict proceedings. Once proceedings have been brought the court dealing with the breach of interdict can make orders for the liberation or further detention of the offending spouse.

(10) The offending spouse is liberated "unless in custody in respect of any other matter."[33] Such other matters would have to be unconnected with the breach of interdict, since the Crown is not entitled to institute criminal proceedings and proceed under section 17 in respect of the same incident.

---

[33] s.17(5)(c).

CHAPTER 6

PROTECTION OF OCCUPANCY RIGHTS AGAINST DEALINGS

6–01. Introduction

In order to protect the statutory occupancy rights of a non-entitled spouse it is necessary to provide against transactions relating to the matrimonial home (such as a sale) which would result in the loss of or prejudice to occupancy rights. The Scottish Law Commission in its Report[1] recommended that a spouse who registered a notice of occupancy rights (a matrimonial home notice) in the Sasine or Land Register could have a subsequent dealing adverse to his or her occupancy rights annulled. The Government in promoting the legislation chose not to follow this recommendation for two reasons. First, registration might provide inadequate protection as spouses might only register a notice after break-up of marriage which could be too late to prevent disposal of the matrimonial home. Secondly, registration would have involved a substantial increase in staff in the Sasine and Land Registers. Instead the Government evolved a scheme whereby the non-entitled spouse is able (except in certain circumstances)[2] to continue to occupy the house in spite of any dealing between the other spouse and a third party. The non-entitled spouse's position is similar to that of a protected tenant. The unfortunate consequence of the decision to create an automatic right rather than one dependent on registration of a notice has been that conveyancing problems have arisen in every house transaction in Scotland. There is no simple way for a purchaser to be certain that there are no occupancy rights in relation to the seller or any previous owner. Hence very great care has to be taken in every case to ensure that the Act's protections against the consequences of unknown occupancy rights are properly invoked. The fact that a university was asked to declare that it did not have a non-entitled spouse is symptomatic of the difficulties created by the scheme chosen.

6–02. An occupancy right is a right to continue to occupy the matrimonial home or to take occupation of it.[3] It is enforceable against those deriving title from the entitled spouse except in the circumstances referred to in paragraphs 6-07 to 6-19 below. Since occupancy rights are conferred upon a non-entitled spouse by statute there is no deed recorded or recordable in the Register of Sasines which will disclose their existence. For the purposes of the Land Register of Scotland an occupancy right is an overriding interest.[4] It therefore overrides or prevails over registered interests in land without registration. Section 6 (4) of the Land Registration (Scotland) Act 1979 empowers the Keeper of the Land Register of Scotland to note any

---

[1] *Occupancy Rights in the Matrimonial Home and Domestic Violence*, Scot. Law Com. No. 60 (1980).
[2] See paras. 6-07 to 6-19.
[3] s.1(1)(a) and (b).
[4] s.6(4)(c).

overriding interest on the title sheet of an interest in land registered in the Land Register, while section 9(4) of that Act permits rectification of that register by noting the existence of an overriding interest. But an occupancy right is not an overriding interest as far as these sections are concerned,[5] so that the Keeper will not note the occupancy rights of the current proprietor's spouse. The title sheet will, however, contain a certificate added by the Keeper that no occupancy rights exist in respect of spouses of previous proprietors, once satisfied that this is indeed the case. The Keeper exercises considerable care in adding this certificate since a third party who relies on it to his or her loss may be able to claim under the indemnity provisions of the Land Registration (Scotland) Act 1979. On first registration the Keeper will therefore require detailed information about every person who has been interested in the property since 1 September 1982, the date of commencement of the Act, or since the five-year "prescription" specified in section 6(3)(*f*) took effect. In addition to consents, renunciations or affidavits, there may have to be evidence that they were produced to a purchaser at the time of the dealing. The vital point to note is that neither the Register of Sasines nor the Land Register of Scotland will disclose the existence of occupancy rights of the current proprietor's spouse. Thus people who propose to enter into a transaction relating to a matrimonial home must satisfy themselves as to the existence of occupancy rights by asking the current proprietor and his or her spouse (if any) or by making inquiries elsewhere.

6–03. General scope of protection

A non-entitled spouse is entitled to continue to occupy the matrimonial home and exercise all the rights conferred by the Act, notwithstanding any dealing by the entitled spouse.[6] Also any third party, who by virtue of such a dealing, would otherwise be entitled to occupy the home is forbidden to do so.[7] This protection exists not only in relation to owner-occupied matrimonial homes but also to tenanted or liferented property. The existence of a non-entitled spouse's occupancy rights has therefore required substantial modifications to previous conveyancing practice where residential property is involved; also landlords must take these rights into account before accepting renunciations of tenancies. It should be noted that the presence or absence of occupancy rights does not affect the validity of a dealing. A purchaser is still the owner even if the seller's spouse can and does exercise occupancy rights. The Act applies to all houses and it would seem that even local authorities and housing associations would be wise to clarify the position of a tenant's spouse before acting on a renunciation of a tenancy.

6–04. Protection will *not* however exist in certain circumstances despite the existence of a spouse of an occupant and it may be very important in practice to take account of this.

Quite apart from cases of renunciation of rights or consent to a dealing, when spouses both have a title to the house or are joint tenants they already have rights of occupancy by virtue of their ownership in common or of their

---

[5] s.6(4)(*a*) and (*b*).
[6] ss.1(1) and 6(1)(*a*).
[7] s.6(1)(*b*).

tenancy. Hence, by virtue of the definition in the first part of section 1(1), neither qualifies as the "non-entitled spouse" on whom statutory occupancy rights are conferred. They may however be entitled to seek court orders regulating occupancy, etc.[8] and have rights to protection under section 9.

If one spouse is merely permitted by a third party to occupy the matrimonial home, or has a title of ownership in common with someone other than the title-holder's spouse (*e.g.* a married brother who owns the home in common with his sister), the spouse of the "permittee" or part-owner does qualify as a non-entitled spouse under section 1(1). There are, therefore, statutory occupancy rights, but these rights are not protected against a dealing by the entitled spouse, as there is a special definition of "entitled spouse" for the purpose of section 6.[9] The ordinary definition does, however, apply for the purposes of heritable securities under section 8.

6–05.   Protection is provided against any dealing capable of prejudicing either directly or indirectly a non-entitled spouse's occupancy rights. Examples of such dealings, for owner-occupied matrimonial homes, are sales, and the granting of leases (whether written or verbal), heritable securities,[9] permissions to occupy and servitudes; and for tenanted homes assignations, renunciations, notices of removal by the tenant, and the granting of sub-leases or permissions to occupy. The creation of a trust (including a trust deed for behoof of creditors) also counts as a dealing. In the original form of the Act, the conclusion of missives of sale probably did fall within the definition of a "dealing," although this caused difficulties in applying the Act, but the time of the dealing is now the date of delivery of the deed.[10] This new definition may itself cause difficulties in cases where entry is given before the title has been granted. A schedule conveyance[11] is not a dealing[12] provided it implements a transaction in respect of which compulsory acquisition powers exist or an acquisition by agreement by a local authority.[13] Giving up a service occupancy on termination of employment probably is not a dealing, nor is a further advance by a building society in reliance on an existing "all sums" security. Bringing an action of division and sale is not a dealing. Protection against this is provided by section 19 (see paragraph 8–01 below). Although doubt has been expressed, it is suggested that the non-entitled spouse's protection does continue even after a second dealing by the person with whom the entitled spouse conducted the first dealing. For example, if occupancy rights survive a sale by the entitled spouse, they will continue to exist even after a further sale by the purchaser, and will be brought to an end only by voluntary action by the non-entitled spouse or by the five-year prescription of unused occupancy rights set out in section 6(3)(*f*).

6–06.   Only voluntary dealings by the entitled spouse are affected. Thus the non-entitled spouse cannot continue to occupy the home where the other spouse is sequestrated and the trustee wishes to sell the home,[14] or the

---

[8] See para. 2-04 above.
[9] s.6(2).
[10] s.6(3)(*e*).
[11] Lands Clauses Consolidation (Scotland) Act 1845, s.80.
[12] s.6(2).
[13] Local Government (Scotland) Act 1973, s.70(3).
[14] See para. 6-21 for contrived sequestrations, and para. 6-19.

landlord irritates the lease, or a creditor adjudges the home and obtains possession,[15] or the home is acquired compulsorily. A sale or other step taken by a heritable creditor to enforce the security is not a dealing of the entitled spouse, even though the creditor's powers arise by virtue of a previous dealing—the grant of the security. The protection which exists against the original grant of a security means that the non-entitled spouse's occupancy rights will be affected only if the granting of the security falls within any of the cases set out in paragraphs 6-08 to 6-14, 6-18 and 6-19 below.

6–07. Exceptions to protection

In any of the situations described in paragraphs 6-08 to 6-19 below the non-entitled spouse's occupancy rights in a matrimonial home are affected by a dealing. In these situations, where the dealing comprises a disposal of the home (*e.g.* a sale or a renunciation of the tenancy) or the grant of a right of occupation (*e.g.* a lease or a sub-lease), the non-entitled spouse is not entitled to continue to occupy the home and the third party is entitled to occupy it. For other dealings such as a sale of part of the home or the grant of a servitude, the non-entitled spouse's occupancy rights are curtailed, and the third party is entitled to exercise the rights acquired by the dealing.

6–08. *Consent by non-entitled spouse (section 6 (3) (a) (i)).* The non-entitled spouse consents to the dealing. A consent must be in writing and in the prescribed form.[16] It is thought that the phrase "the non-entitled spouse" merely identifies the person whose consent is required and does not mean that a spouse must be non-entitled at the time of giving consent. Indeed the latter interpretation would have unfortunate and surely unintended consequences since a wife whose husband was buying a new home for the family with the aid of a loan would be unable to consent to the granting of the security until after settlement when her husband becomes entitled to occupy the home, and thus the loan would not be available for settlement. Where the spouses are estranged consent should be sought before the dealing commences, otherwise any preliminary expenditure may be wasted. It would be prudent for the entitled spouse to obtain consent before entering into a binding obligation; the third party too would probably wish to see consent at this stage so that he or she can be sure the dealing will go through. But where the couple are happily married and have discussed the dealing together the consent could well be left to the final stages and might be incorporated in the deed implementing the dealing. If the consent is not incorporated in a recorded deed registration in the Books of Council and Session will preserve it for future reference; alternatively it could be put up with the titles. The consent might be given even after the dealing has taken place, although this is not good practice as the purchaser's statutory protection depends upon the consent being produced "at the time of the dealing". However a consent given after the dealing would be likely to justify a plea of personal bar against the non-entitled spouse who granted it if there were to be an attempt to enforce occupancy rights. It would also seem to be effective under section 6(3)(*a*)(i) and (ii) where no time limit is specified. An apparently valid consent

[15] See para.6-21 for contrived adjudications.
[16] S.I. 1982 No. 971. See Appendix III.

which is a forgery or otherwise invalid is not effective except in relation to a sale to a good faith purchaser[17] or a heritable security granted to a good faith creditor.[18]

6–09. *Renunciation by non-entitled spouse (section 6 (3) (a) (ii)).* The non-entitled spouse renounces his or her occupancy rights in the matrimonial home to which the dealing relates. Normally the non-entitled spouse will have renounced before the dealing commences, but he or she may renounce during the course of the dealing or after it has taken place. It is thought that the phrase "non-entitled spouse" merely identifies the person whose renunciation is required. A renunciation by a person who is a spouse at the time of renunciation must comply with the requirements of section 1(5) and (6), but a renunciation by a fiancé(e) in general terms and not "notarised" is effective so long as it is in writing. An apparently valid renunciation which is a forgery or otherwise invalid is not effective except in relation to a sale to a good faith purchaser[19] or a heritable security granted to a good faith creditor.[20]

6–10. *Consent dispensed with (section 6 (3) (b)).* The court has dispensed with the consent of the non-entitled spouse to the particular dealing. The situations in which the court may dispense with consent are set out in section 7 (1). Consent may be dispensed with in connection with a proposed dealing or with a dealing which has taken place. It has been suggested that a proposed dealing means a dealing (completed or incomplete) with a particular third party rather than a general proposal to deal.[20a] Either the entitled spouse or a third party who is prejudiced by the lack of consent may apply to the court for a dispensing order. The power to dispense with consent is discretionary, and, in deciding whether to grant an order, the court is required to consider all the circumstances of the case and in particular the conduct of the spouses, their needs and resources, the needs of any child of the family, any business use of the home and whether the entitled spouse has offered the non-entitled spouse suitable alternative accommodation.[21] It should be noted that the provisions of section 5 of the Married Women's Property (Scotland) Act 1881 (which empower the court to dispense with the husband's consent to any dealing by his minor wife where she has been deserted or is living apart from him with his consent) have been repealed.[22]

6–11. The main ground on which the court can dispense with consent is that the non-entitled spouse is withholding consent unreasonably.[23] What is unreasonable will depend on the particular circumstances in each case. A wife who refuses consent to a sale because she does not want to move to a new home on her husband obtaining employment elsewhere would no doubt be regarded as unreasonable. It would be otherwise if the sale was simply to raise money and no alternative accommodation was offered to her. In two

[17] s.6(3)(*e*)(ii).
[18] s.8(2)(*b*) and (2A)(*b*).
[19] s.6(3)(*e*)(ii).
[20] s.8(2)(*b*) and (2A)(*b*).
[20a] *Dunsmore* v. *Dunsmore*, 1986 S.L.T. (Sh. Ct.) 9.
[21] s.7(3). For discussion of the procedure see *Longmuir* v. *Longmuir*, 1985 S.L.T. (Sh. Ct.) 33.
[22] Family Law (Scotland) Act 1985, s.28(2) and Sched. 2.
[23] s.7(1)(*a*)—see *Perkins* v. *Perkins*, Glasgow Sheriff Court, 11 December 1984 (unreported).

situations the non-entitled spouse will be taken to be withholding consent unreasonably. First, where the non-entitled spouse has led his or her spouse to believe that consent would be given and there has been no material change in circumstances since then.[24] For example, a husband may proceed with the sale of the home relying on his wife's verbal consent or her tacit approval of the purchase of a new home. If the wife subsequently refused to sign the prescribed form of consent she would be taken to be withholding consent unreasonably. Secondly, where the entitled spouse is unable to obtain an answer to a request for consent despite having taken all reasonable steps to obtain the consent.[25] This has the odd consequence that a non-entitled spouse is in a worse position by refusing to answer a request for consent than by refusing consent.

6–12. The other grounds on which the court may dispense with the consent of a non-entitled spouse are that the non-entitled spouse is unable to consent by reason of physical or mental disability,[26] the non-entitled spouse cannot be found after reasonable steps have been taken to trace him or her[27] or the non-entitled spouse is a minor.[28]

6–13. *Antenuptial dealings and obligations (section 6 (3) (c)).* The actual dealing may have occurred before the marriage of the non-entitled spouse to the entitled spouse. The only dealings in this category which are likely to affect occupancy rights are grants of heritable securities or trust deeds containing a power of sale and in both cases the power to sell the property which has become a matrimonial home can be exercised after marriage without regard to the non-entitled spouse's occupancy rights. A dealing takes place only at the date of delivery to a purchaser of the deed transferring title.[29] However, although this date may be after marriage, the dealing may proceed without any need for consent or renunciation by the non-entitled spouse if there was in existence before the marriage a binding obligation to complete the dealing. A common example would be that the wife's consent, etc., is not required if her husband had concluded missives of sale prior to the marriage, but the possible situations are not limited to short-term transitional transactions. For instance, an option to purchase might have been given many years before the marriage, or the entitled spouse might have been the beneficiary of a gift of the house subject to a condition of onward conveyance in certain events. Similarly, missives may have been concluded before the marriage with a suspensive condition (such as obtaining planning permission) which is purified after the marriage by the purchaser. In all such cases of antenuptial dealings—and also in the similar transitional provisions for pre-Act dealings—it will be highly desirable to keep with the titles dated missives and, if appropriate, a marriage certificate. A subsequent purchaser, or the Keeper of the Registers, may require proof that the obligation arose before the relevant date.

---

[24] s.7(2)(*a*).
[25] s.7(2)(*b*).
[26] s.7(1)(*b*).
[27] s.7(1)(*c*).
[28] s.7(1)(*d*).
[29] s.6(3)(*e*) at the end.

6-14. *Pre-Act dealings and obligations (section 6 (3)(d)).* The dealing occurred before the Act came into force on 1 September 1982. A power of sale under a heritable security or a trust deed granted before this date may be exercised afterwards without regard to the non-entitled spouse's occupancy rights. There is also a transitional provision similar to that in the preceding paragraph; the relevant date is the date the Act came into force (1 September 1982) instead of the date of marriage.

6-15. *Protection of the good faith purchaser (section 6 (3) (e)).* A non-entitled spouse cannot continue to exercise his or her occupancy rights in a matrimonial home after it has been sold by the entitled spouse as long as the following conditions are met. First, the purchaser acts in good faith. The purchaser (or his or her solicitor) must have made reasonable inquiries about the existence of a non-entitled spouse, and have no knowledge casting doubt on the truth of the answers received. Secondly, the seller produces an affidavit that the subjects of sale are not a matrimonial home in relation to which a spouse of the seller has occupancy rights, or produces an apparently valid consent or renunciation of occupancy rights by the non-entitled spouse. The affidavit should be declared as near as conveniently possible to the date of settlement since acceptance of an old affidavit might suggest bad faith. The purchaser need not "go behind" a consent or renunciation provided it appears to meet the legal requirements for validity,[30] unless of course he or she is aware of something which casts doubt on the validity. So long as the purchaser is in good faith he or she is protected by the affidavit against any occupancy rights, irrespective of the truth or falsity of the affidavit.[31]

As a result of the amendments effected by the Law Reform (Miscellaneous Provisions) (Scotland) Act 1985, the affidavit, renunciation or consent must now be produced at "or before" the time of the dealing, and the time of the dealing is defined as the date of delivery to the purchaser of the deed transferring title. This would seem to mean that later affidavits or other deeds would not give the statutory protection of section 6(3)(e) to the purchaser, although a renunciation or consent may still receive effect under section 6(3)(a). As before, however, prudent purchasers will insist on having the documents by the time of settlement at latest. The question whether the good faith purchaser protection applied only to purchases of the whole matrimonial home has been resolved by the new wording of section 6(3)(e), which now applies to any sale to a third party.

An affidavit is to be sworn or affirmed "by the seller." It would not seem to be competent for an affidavit to be executed by an attorney for the seller, as an attorney would not be capable of swearing an oath on the seller's behalf. An affidavit will have to be sworn or affirmed before a notary public acting as such. This is already specified for renunciations by section 1(6) but seems to apply to affidavits also, because there is no express authority for justices of the peace to receive such affidavits.[32] Affidavits are exempt from stamp duty.[33]

---

[30] See paras. 6-08 and 6-09 above.
[31] See "Affidavits and the Matrimonial Homes Act" (1982) 27 J.L.S. 455.
[32] Statutory Declarations Act 1835, s.13.
[33] Finance Act 1949, s.35.

It will be noted that the protection of section 6(3)(*e*) applies only to a "sale to a third party." A gift would not be a sale and hence would not be protected, but the question of simulated sale at a nominal price would be met by the requirement of good faith. It is suggested that an excambion in good faith would qualify as a sale for this purpose.

6–16. The provisions of section 6(3)(*e*) are in addition to, not in substitution for, the other provisions of section 6(3). Thus a purchaser is protected by a decree dispensing with consent or a valid consent or renunciation even though he or she is in bad faith or the documents were produced long after the dealing had taken place. If the apparently valid affidavit, consent or renunciation is forged or otherwise invalid the non-entitled spouse cannot continue to occupy the home but he or she may have a claim for compensation under section 3(7) against the entitled spouse. The entitled spouse may also be liable to prosecution for swearing a false affidavit or committing forgery.

6–17. *Prescription of unused occupancy rights (section 6(3)(f)).* If the occupancy rights of a non-entitled spouse have not been validly excluded, they are not affected by any dealing by the entitled spouse. The non-entitled spouse does not require to be already in occupation in order to enforce occupancy rights. Hence such a non-entitled spouse is in a position to enforce occupancy rights (and in practice to evict the current occupant) even against the third or fourth owner after the dealing by the entitled spouse. One of the great fears of conveyancers has been that the spouse of any of the previous owners might be in a position to do this, and to protect the current owner it is therefore necessary to ensure that occupancy rights cannot have survived the ownership of *any* previous title-holder. Where the title is or is to be registered in the Land Register the Keeper's certificate may include a guarantee against occupancy rights of the spouses of all owners before the current seller, but in other cases the risk continues.

To meet this, the Law Reform (Miscellaneous Provisions) (Scotland) Act 1985 has introduced a five-year prescription of unexercised occupancy rights. This now appears as section 6(3)(*f*) of the Matrimonial Homes Act and probably has effect as a limitation rather than an extinctive prescription. Where the entitled spouse has permanently ceased to be entitled to occupy the matrimonial home (*e.g.* after a sale) and at any time thereafter a continuous period of five years has elapsed during which the non-entitled spouse has not occupied the matrimonial home, the non-entitled spouse's occupancy rights are no longer a threat to the current owner's possession as they are no longer protected against the consequences of the entitled spouse's dealing. There had been pressure for a prescriptive period of only two years, which might have been a reasonable balance between protection of the non-entitled spouse and the legitimate interests of a purchaser, but five years was the final figure. It will be noted that there is no requirement for this purpose that the purchaser must be in good faith.

6–18. *Protection of heritable creditors in good faith (section 8).* A heritable creditor who takes a security over a matrimonial home after the Act came into force on 1 September 1982[34] is entitled to exercise his or her rights under the security (and in particular the power of sale) free from the constraints of the occupancy rights of the non-entitled spouse if the conditions of section 8 are complied with. There are now separate provisions for cases where the security was granted from 1 September 1982 to 29 December 1985 inclusive, and for securities granted on or after 30 December 1985 (when section 13 of the Law Reform (Miscellaneous Provisions) (Scotland) Act 1985 came into force).

In both cases the security must have been granted by the entitled spouse (irrespective of whether that spouse is the debtor) and the creditor granting the loan must have acted in good faith. A collusive arrangement between the creditor and the entitled spouse would establish lack of good faith. In both situations also, the time of granting a security is the date of delivery of the deed creating the security.[35]

For securities granted before 30 December 1985, the entitled spouse must have produced to the lender either an affidavit that there is no non-entitled spouse or an apparently valid consent or renunciation by the non-entitled spouse. These documents must have been produced "before the granting of the loan," which seems to mean the time when the money lent is made over.

For securities granted on or after 30 December 1985, there must be produced to the lender, "at or before the granting of the security," an affidavit that the security subjects are not a matrimonial home in relation to which a spouse of the grantor has occupancy rights, or an apparently valid consent or renunciation. It will be noted that the relevant point of time is now the granting of the security rather than of the loan, and that the documents may be produced at that time and not necessarily before it.

So long as the security was granted after the Act came into force, and the appropriate protective steps have been taken by the creditor, section 8(1) also gives the court power to order a non-entitled spouse in sole occupation of the matrimonial home to maintain any payments due under the secured loan. This might for example be significant after an exclusion order.

6–19.   The provisions of section 8 are in addition to, and not in substitution for, the general provisions of section 6(3).[36] From 30 December 1985 a creditor taking a security for prior indebtedness will be able to rely on the provisions of section 8(2A), as the documents can be produced at the granting of the security, though not before the granting of the loan. In cases of securities for prior indebtedness taken before 30 December 1985 the creditor has to rely on section 6(3)(*a*), and on a consent or renunciation from the borrower's (or guarantor's) spouse.

A further advance made under a security for all sums due and to become due does not require a consent, renunciation or affidavit to be obtained anew. Such an advance is not a dealing in its own right, as it merely takes advantage of the provisions of the existing dealing, the security.

---

[34] See para. 6-14 for securities granted before 1 September 1982.
[35] s.8(2B).
[36] s.6(3)(*e*) is, of course, limited to sales of the matrimonial home.

Sequestration coupled with the trustee requiring vacant possession terminates the entitlement of the bankrupt entitled spouse. As this is not a dealing by the entitled spouse, it also terminates the occupancy rights of the non-entitled spouse. However, when the Bankruptcy (Scotland) Act 1985 comes into force on 1 April 1986, the basis of the protective measures for the spouse will be different. If the debtor's estate includes a matrimonial home of which the debtor was an entitled spouse and the other spouse is a non-entitled spouse, the permanent trustee will be required to inform the non-entitled spouse of the award of sequestration, of the non-entitled spouse's right to petition for recall of the sequestration, and of the Court of Session's power to protect occupancy rights against contrived sequestrations.[37] In addition the permanent trustee under the 1985 Act will require to obtain the consent of the debtor's spouse or former spouse resident in the "family home" or obtain the court's authority before any sale or disposal of the family home can be carried through. As most matrimonial homes will also be family homes within the definition in section 40(4)(*a*) of the Bankruptcy Act, there will be a further measure of protection of a non-entitled spouse, even although occupancy rights as such are ineffective.

Subject to this further protection when the 1985 Act comes into force, sequestration might be a creditor's only way of obtaining vacant possession of a matrimonial home owned by a spouse who has taken over liability as debtor under a security granted by a previous proprietor after the Matrimonial Homes Act came into force. However, the acceptance of liability would probably be regarded as a dealing by the present owner, and in that case consent or renunciation by the non-entitled spouse would be necessary before the creditor could enforce his or her security. In such cases it would be at least desirable that the security should be discharged and a fresh security taken from the new entitled spouse.

6–20. Jointly entitled spouses

The protection afforded to a non-entitled spouse by section 6 is extended to jointly entitled spouses by section 9. This is necessary because certain dealings by one jointly entitled spouse prejudice the occupancy rights of the other. A common tenancy continued by tacit relocation can be brought to an end for both co-tenants by a notice of removal given by one, while a sale by one spouse of his or her undivided share results in the other spouse sharing the matrimonial home with the purchaser. Although the dealing will be valid between the parties to it, the other spouse's rights will not be affected, and the third party will not be able to take occupation unless the consent of the non-dealing spouse is obtained or another provision of section 6(3) applies. It should be stressed that only dealings by one of the jointly entitled couple are affected by section 9; where both spouses enter into a transaction relating to the matrimonial home together no consent from either spouse is necessary.

6–21. Contrived diligences

An entitled spouse could circumvent the non-entitled spouse's occupancy rights by arranging his or her own sequestration or having the matrimonial home adjudged by a creditor. The protection afforded to the non-entitled

---

[37] Bankruptcy (Scotland) Act 1985, s.41(1). See para. 6-21 below.

spouse by section 6 does not apply for these are not dealings of the entitled spouse. To prevent such contrivances the Court of Session is empowered, on petition by the non-entitled spouse, to recall the sequestration[38] or adjudication[39] or to make other orders to protect the occupancy rights (*e.g.* postponing a sale by the trustee in sequestration or preventing an adjudger from obtaining vacant possession). These powers are exercised where the court is satisfied that the purpose of the sequestration or adjudication was wholly or mainly to defeat the occupancy rights of the petitioner. "Satisfied" may be interpreted as requiring proof even where the petition is unopposed. The purpose of any sequestration is, of course, to realise the value of the matrimonial home for the benefit of creditors and this necessarily means defeating the occupancy rights of the spouse. In order to succeed the petitioner has to show that the entitled spouse played an active part in the sequestration or adjudication and there was collusion between the entitled spouse and his or her creditor(s).

6–22. Practice in sales

Although the Act only applies to matrimonial homes it is prudent practice to treat any residential property as a matrimonial home, at least until clear evidence to the contrary is produced. Purchasers will obviously require to satisfy themselves that no occupancy rights arise from the spouse of the current proprietor. It is suggested that purchasers should examine all sales since the Act came into force which fall within the "prescriptive" period of section 6(3)(*f*), in order to protect themselves against any subsequent assertion of occupancy rights. Since an occupancy right does not prejudice title, positive prescription will not operate to give a title free of occupancy rights. An unfortunate purchaser might have to buy another house, although he or she may be entitled to be indemnified by the Keeper of the Land Register of Scotland if the title sheet contained a note[40] which wrongly stated that there were no occupancy rights in respect of spouses of previous proprietors. The following table indicates the main points to consider in the case of a sale.

---

[38] s.10 and Bankruptcy (Scotland) Act 1913, s.31A. From 1 April 1986 Bankruptcy (Scotland) Act 1985, s.41(1).
[39] s.12.
[40] See para. 6-02. No indemnity exists where the title is recorded in the Register of Sasines.

Seller	*Purchaser*
Ask spouse for consent to proposed sale, preferably before any steps are taken and certainly before missives are concluded.	Stipulate in missives for vacant possession unencumbered by occupancy rights of any non-entitled spouse whether of the current or a previous proprietor. Include a provision for the stipulation to remain in effect, notwithstanding delivery of the disposition.[41]
If no consent apply to the court for consent to be dispensed with (or abandon the sale).	
Obtain spouse's consent in prescribed form, or produce renunciation by spouse or swear an affidavit under section 6(3)(*e*).	Make inquiries as to the existence of a spouse where the title of the property is in the name of an individual.
	At settlement obtain an up-to-date affidavit, a consent, a court decree dispensing with consent or a renunciation of occupancy rights.
	If title is to be registered in the Land Register, send the affidavit, consent, court decree or renunciation to the Keeper. Check that a note of non-existence of occupancy rights is added.

---

[41] *Winston v. Patrick,* 1981 S.L.T. 41; 1980 S.C. 246.

CHAPTER 7

COHABITING COUPLES

7–01. Introduction

Many of the rights conferred on non-entitled spouses are extended to non-entitled cohabiting partners by section 18. In contrast to a spouse whose occupancy rights arise by operation of law by virtue of marriage, a cohabiting partner only has occupancy rights if the court on application makes an order to this effect.

7–02. Occupancy rights

A cohabiting partner who is not otherwise entitled or permitted to occupy the house and whose partner is so entitled or permitted may (unless the right to apply has been renounced) apply to the court for an order granting occupancy rights in that house. However, unless and until a court order has actually granted these occupancy rights, a non-entitled cohabitee has no rights at all under the Act. A cohabitee is not in the same position as a spouse, and thus if the partner who is entitled withdraws the other's permission to live in the house, the non-entitled cohabitee would have to go to the court seeking an order under section 18 on pain of removal by an action of ejection. Where the applicant's partner is entitled or permitted to occupy the house together with a person other than the applicant, occupancy rights can be applied for only if that other person has waived (either expressly or by implication) his or her right of occupancy.[1]

7–03.   An order granting occupancy rights is made only where the applicant and his or her partner are living together as if they were man and wife. Section 18(2) provides the court with some guidance as to the interpretation of these words. The court is directed to have regard to the duration of the cohabitation and the existence of children of the relationship. Other relevant factors might include whether the couple are a single household or merely live together in order to share expenses (*e.g.* flatmates), and how the couple regard themselves and represent their relationship to their friends.

7–04.   It is not necessary that the couple are living together as if they were man and wife at the date of the application. Indeed such an interpretation would deny effect to the provisions, for many applications will be made only on break-up of the relationship when the couple have separated. However, although the court has jurisdiction, it might decide on the merits that it would be inappropriate to exercise its discretionary powers after some months of separation.[2]

---

[1] s.18(6), echoing s.1(2).
[2] *O'Neill* v. *Williams* (1984) 14 Fam. Law 85, construing a similar provision in the Domestic Violence and Matrimonial Proceedings Act 1976.

7–05. Occupancy rights can be granted only in respect of the house in which a couple are (or were recently) cohabiting. House includes any dwelling, a caravan (whether fixed or mobile), a houseboat or other structure, and the occupancy rights extend to the garden and other buildings.[3] The differences between a cohabitee's house and a matrimonial home should be noted.[4] Thus a property remains a matrimonial home even though the spouses have separated some time ago; and neither spouse need have lived in a house for it to become a matrimonial home as long as it was acquired as a family home.

7–06. Duration of occupancy rights

Occupancy rights can be granted initially only for a period not exceeding six months.[5] Thereafter the non-entitled partner may apply to the court for a renewal and the court is empowered to grant occupancy rights for further periods of up to six months at a time.[6] No guidance is given as to how the court should exercise its discretion to renew. Failure on the part of the non-entitled partner to obtain alternative accommodation might justify renewal, as might the undesirability of moving children shortly before important school examinations. Although it is possible for a non-entitled partner, by repeated applications, to obtain indefinite occupancy of the house, courts will adopt this approach only in very special circumstances, since the entitled partner might be thus permanently prevented from enjoying his or her own property or disposing of it. A court order granting occupancy rights to a non-entitled partner lapses automatically when the other partner ceases to be entitled. For example, it lapses on the entitled partner's death, the house being disposed of or the lease being irritated.

7–07. Other rights

During the period for which occupancy rights have been granted a non-entitled partner can exercise the subsidiary rights under section 2 and apply to the court for orders under sections 2, 3 and 4. Orders such as an exclusion order or an order granting use and possession of furniture and plenishings and ancillary interdicts may well be applied for at the same time as the initial grant of occupancy is sought. A non-entitled partner with occupancy rights can apply for a tenancy transfer order and a power of arrest can be attached to any interdict that would rank as a matrimonial interdict had the partners been spouses. All these rights are also available to either partner where both are entitled or permitted to occupy the house.

7–08. Protection of occupancy rights against dealings

Sections 6 to 9 relating to the protection of occupancy rights against dealings with third parties, do not apply to cohabiting couples.[7] The occupancy rights granted to a non-entitled partner will therefore be prejudiced or defeated by a dealing relating to the house.[8] A non-entitled partner can obtain a measure of protection by applying to the court for an

---

[3] s.18(6).
[4] See paras. 2-13 to 2-21 above.
[5] Before 30 December 1985, the period was three months.
[6] s.18(1).
[7] s.18(3).
[8] s.18(5).

interdict[9] prohibiting the entitled partner from entering into any voluntary dealing while occupancy rights subsist. In appropriate cases this interdict should be applied for at the same time as the application for occupancy rights is made. Even if no interdict is obtained, an entitled partner who disposes of the house while his or her partner has occupancy rights will be liable to pay compensation or damages.[10] An application for compensation must be made while the court order granting occupancy rights is in force.

7–09. The provisions to avoid the effect of contrived sequestrations and adjudications do not apply to cohabiting couples.[11]

7–10. Differences between cohabiting couples and spouses

The major differences between spouses and cohabiting couples have been dealt with in the preceding paragraphs. The following differences should also be noted:

(a) In the case of spouses the needs and interests of any child of the family have to be considered in certain applications,[12] and an exclusion order may be granted to protect a child of the family.[13] Where a cohabiting couple is concerned the expression used is "any child residing with the cohabiting couple." This is to some extent wider than "child of the family"[14] for it includes an au-pair or a foster child staying with the couple; on the other hand it is narrower because the child must be residing (or perhaps have been recently residing) with the couple at the relevant date.

(b) For cohabiting couples where one partner is entitled and the other non-entitled an application for apportionment of expenditure on the house or furniture and plenishings can be made only while the non-entitled partner has occupancy rights, even though the applicant is the entitled partner.[15] Where both partners are entitled the application must be made while they remain jointly entitled and not later than five years from the date on which the expenditure was incurred.[16] An application by a spouse, however, may be made at any time within the five-year period.[17]

(c) An order under section 3 or 4 terminates automatically when the non-entitled partner's occupancy rights terminate, unless the court in granting the order specified earlier termination,[18] but where both partners are entitled any order lasts until recall.[19] In the case of spouses an order terminates when the marriage comes to an end.[20] Disposal of a cohabiting couple's house by the entitled partner terminates any order relating to it,[21] but an order relating to a matrimonial home only terminates if the disposal by the entitled spouse is in accordance with sections 6 and 7.[22]

---

9 Under s.3(1)(*e*).
10 See para. 2-48 above.
11 s.18(3) and ss. 10 and 12. From 1 April 1986, Bankruptcy (Scotland) Act 1985, s.41.
12 ss.3(3), 4(3)(*a*), 7(3), 13(3) and 19.
13 s.4(2).
14 s.22 and see para. 3-17 above.
15 s.18(3) as read with s.2(3) and (5)(*b*).
16 s.18(3) as read with s.2(4)(*b*), (5)(*b*) and (7).
17 s.2(7).
18 s.18(4)(*a*).
19 s.18(4)(*b*).
20 s.5(1)(*a*), but the court has power to regulate occupation after divorce: Family Law (Scotland) Act 1985, s.14(2).
21 s.18(5).
22 s.5(1)(*b*) and see para. 2-52 above.

(d) A power of arrest lapses on termination of the non-entitled partner's occupancy rights whether that partner is the holder of the interdict or the interdicted partner.[23] If both partners are entitled the power of arrest lasts as long as they remain jointly entitled unless recalled earlier.[24] For spouses a power of arrest terminates with the marriage unless previously recalled.[25] Note, however, that a power of arrest can be attached only to a matrimonial interdict. The result is that a cohabitee who is entitled can obtain an interdict with power of arrest attached only if his or her partner had previously applied for, and had been granted, occupancy rights.

(e) A heritable creditor cannot apply to the court for an order requiring a resident non-entitled partner to make payments due under the security by the absent entitled partner, since section 8 does not apply to cohabiting couples.[26]

(f) The court has no power to deal with a contrived poinding where a cohabiting partner has a use and possession order, since section 11 does not apply to cohabiting couples.[27]

(g) The court has no power to refuse or delay a decree of division and sale of a house owned in common by a cohabiting couple, since section 19 only applies to spouses.[28]

(h) A non-entitled partner's consent is not required to the entitled partner's agreement to shorten or dispense with the period for complying with the requirements of a calling-up notice or a notice of default, since section 20 only applies to spouses.[29]

7-11. Homelessness

In *McAlinden* v. *Bearsden and Milngavie District Council*[30] it was held that a cohabiting partner who chose not to avail herself of the right under section 18 of the Matrimonial Homes Act to apply for occupancy rights in her former partner's home was not homeless within the meaning of section 1 of the Housing (Homeless Persons) Act 1977, and further that the council's decision to that effect was not one which no reasonable authority could have reached. The same reasoning may apply to spouses who chose not to exercise their statutory occupancy rights or use other legal remedies.

---

[23] s.18(3) as read with s.15.
[24] s.18(3) as read with s.15.
[25] s.15(2).
[26] s.18(3).
[27] s.18(3).
[28] s.18(3).
[29] s.18(3).
[30] 1986 S.L.T. 191.

CHAPTER 8

MISCELLANEOUS

8–01. Division and sale of matrimonial homes

Where the spouses own a matrimonial home in common, each could under the previous law force a sale of the property by applying to the court for a decree of division and sale unless they had agreed not to do so. Section 19 provides that in any such application the court may either refuse to grant decree, postpone the granting of decree, or grant decree subject to conditions. In exercising these powers the court is enjoined to consider all the circumstances of the case, in particular the conduct of the spouses, their needs and resources, the needs of any child of the family, any business use of the home, and whether the spouse seeking decree has offered suitable alternative accommodation to the other spouse. These powers might be used to prevent or delay disposal of the matrimonial home while the children are dependent, or to allow a spouse who carries on a business in the home time to find alternative premises. These powers cannot be exercised after divorce, but it seems that so long as the action is brought (or possibly, the court's decree is granted) during the subsistence of the marriage, any postponement or conditions decided upon by the court may continue in being after the dissolution of the marriage. Hence it was not incompetent to seek postponement of the decree of division and sale until a child attained the age of 18, even although that date would be some considerable time after the likely date of a decree of divorce.[1] Bringing an action of division and sale is not a dealing in respect of which the other spouse's consent may be dispensed with.[2] The court's powers do not apply in the case of cohabiting couples.[3]

8–02. Consent in relation to calling up standard securities

Section 20 provides that where the debtor is married and the security is over a matrimonial home, he or she may not agree to shorten or dispense with the period for complying with the requirements of a calling-up notice[4] or a notice of default,[5] without the consent of the other spouse. Securities granted before the Act came into force are affected as well as securities granted afterwards. In the latter case the non-entitled spouse's consent could be incorporated in the security itself.

8–03. Jurisdiction

In general any application or action under the Act may be brought in either the Court of Session or the sheriff courts. But the Court of Session has exclusive jurisdiction in relation to contrived sequestrations or adjudications;

---

[1] *Crow* v. *Crow*, Outer House, 15 August 1985, unreported but noted in (1985) 30 J.L.S. 461.
[2] *Dunsmore* v. *Dunsmore*, 1986 S.L.T. (Sh. Ct.) 9.
[3] Para. 7-10 above.
[4] Conveyancing and Feudal Reform (Scotland) Act 1970, s.19.
[5] 1970 Act, s.21.

while the sheriff courts have exclusive jurisdiction in relation to contrived poindings. The sheriff courts will probably be the choice of most litigants unless consistorial proceedings are pending in the Court of Session. The sheriff, in proceedings under the Act, has jurisdiction if the matrimonial home or a cohabiting couple's house is situated within the sheriffdom, in addition to the other grounds of jurisdiction contained in section 6 of the Sheriff Courts (Scotland) Act 1907.

8–04. Vexatious proceedings

Section 21 disapplies section 2(2) of the Law Reform (Husband and Wife) Act 1962 (which empowers the court to dismiss proceedings in respect of any wrongful act or omission or for the prevention of any wrongful act if it appears that no substantial advantage would accrue to either spouse) to any proceedings brought under the Act. Thus a spouse cannot be prevented from making vexatious or trivial applications for compensation for loss of occupancy rights or for apportionment of expenditure. Such conduct is deterred by the courts, in the exercise of their discretionary powers, refusing to grant the application and awarding expenses against the applicant. More serious conduct could also be deterred under the Vexatious Actions (Scotland) Act 1898.

APPENDIX I

Matrimonial Homes (Family Protection) (Scotland) Act 1981

(1981 c. 59)

ARRANGEMENT OF SECTIONS

An Act to make new provision for Scotland as to the rights of occupancy of spouses in a matrimonial home and of cohabiting couples in the house where they cohabit; to provide for the transfer of the tenancy of a matrimonial home between the spouses in certain circumstances during marriage and on granting decree of divorce or nullity of marriage, and for the transfer of the tenancy of a house occupied by a cohabiting couple between the partners in certain circumstances; to strengthen the law relating to matrimonial interdicts; and for connected purposes.

[30th October 1981]

Protection of occupancy rights of one spouse against the other

Right of spouse without title to occupy matrimonial home

[1] **1.**—(1) Where, apart from the provisions of this Act, one spouse is entitled, or permitted by a third party, to occupy a matrimonial home (an "entitled spouse") and the other spouse is not so entitled or permitted (a "non-entitled spouse"), the non-entitled spouse shall, subject to the provisions of this Act, have the following rights—

  (a) if in occupation, a right to continue to occupy the matrimonial home;

  (b) if not in occupation, a right to enter into and occupy the matrimonial home.

(1A) The rights conferred by subsection (1) above to continue to occupy or, as the case may be, to enter and occupy the matrimonial home include, without prejudice to their generality, the right to do so together with any child of the family.

(2) In subsection (1) above, an "entitled spouse" includes a spouse who is entitled, or permitted by a third party, to occupy a matrimonial home along with an individual who is not the other spouse only if that individual has waived his or her right of occupation in favour of the spouse so entitled or permitted.

(3) If the entitled spouse refuses to allow the non-entitled spouse to exercise the right conferred by subsection (1)(b) above, the non-entitled spouse may exercise that right only with the leave of the court under section 3(3) or (4) of this Act.

(4) In this Act, the rights mentioned in paragraphs (a) and (b) of subsection (1) above are referred to as occupancy rights.

(5) A non-entitled spouse may renounce in writing his or her occupancy rights only—

  (a) in a particular matrimonial home; or

  (b) in a particular property which it is intended by the spouses will become a matrimonial home.

(6) A renunciation under subsection (5) above shall have effect only if at the time of making the renunciation, the non-entitled spouse has sworn or affirmed before a notary public that it was made freely and without coercion of any kind. In this subsection, "notary public" includes any person duly authorised by the law of the country (other than Scotland) in which the swearing or affirmation takes place to administer oaths or receive affirmations in that other country.

NOTE
[1] As amended by the Law Reform (Miscellaneous Provisions) (Scotland) Act 1985, s. 13 (2), (3) and (4).

Subsidiary and consequential rights

[1] **2.**—(1) For the purpose of securing the occupancy rights of a non-entitled spouse, that spouse shall, in relation to a matrimonial home, be entitled without the consent of the entitled spouse—

  (a) to make any payment due by the entitled spouse in respect of rent, rates, secured loan instalments, interest or other outgoings (not being outgoings on repairs or improvements);

  (b) to perform any other obligation incumbent on the entitled spouse (not being an obligation in respect of non-essential repairs or improvements);

  (c) to enforce performance of an obligation by a third party which that third party has undertaken to the entitled spouse to the extent that the entitled spouse may enforce such performance;

(*d*) to carry out such essential repairs as the entitled spouse may carry out;

(*e*) to carry out such non-essential repairs or improvements as may be authorised by an order of the court, being such repairs or improvements as the entitled spouse may carry out and which the court considers to be appropriate for the reasonable enjoyment of the occupancy rights;

(*f*) to take such other steps, for the purpose of protecting the occupancy rights of the non-entitled spouse, as the entitled spouse may take to protect the occupancy rights of the entitled spouse.

(2) Any payment made under subsection (1)(*a*) above or any obligation performed under subsection (1)(*b*) above shall have effect in relation to the rights of a third party as if the payment were made or the obligation were performed by the entitled spouse; and the performance of an obligation which has been enforced under subsection (1)(*c*) above shall have effect as if it had been enforced by the entitled spouse.

(3) Where there is an entitled and a non-entitled spouse, the court, on the application of either of them, may, having regard in particular to the respective financial circumstances of the spouses, make an order apportioning expenditure incurred or to be incurred by either spouse—

(*a*) without the consent of the other spouse, on any of the items mentioned in paragraphs (*a*) and (*d*) of subsection (1) above;

(*b*) with the consent of the other spouse, on anything relating to a matrimonial home.

(4) Where both spouses are entitled, or permitted by a third party, to occupy a matrimonial home—

(*a*) either spouse shall be entitled, without the consent of the other spouse, to carry out such non-essential repairs or improvements as may be authorised by an order of the court, being such repairs or improvements as the court considers to be appropriate for the reasonable enjoyment of the occupancy rights;

(*b*) the court, on the application of either spouse, may, having regard in particular to the respective financial circumstances of the spouses, make an order apportioning expenditure incurred or to be incurred by either spouse, with or without the consent of the other spouse, on anything relating to the matrimonial home.

(5) Where one spouse owns or hires, or is acquiring under a hire-purchase or conditional sale agreement, furniture and plenishings in a matrimonial home—

(*a*) the other spouse may, without the consent of the first mentioned spouse—

(i) make any payment due by the first mentioned spouse which is necessary, or take any other step which the first mentioned spouse is entitled to take, to secure the possession or use of any such furniture and plenishings (and any such payment shall have effect in relation to the rights of a third party as if it were made by the first mentioned spouse); or

(ii) carry out such essential repairs to the furniture and plenishings as the first mentioned spouse is entitled to carry out;

(*b*) the court, on the application of either spouse, may, having regard in particular to the respective financial circumstances of the spouses, make an order apportioning expenditure incurred or to be incurred by either spouse—

(i)   without the consent of the other spouse, in making payments under a hire, hire-purchase or conditional sale agreement, or in paying interest charges in respect of the furniture and plenishings, or in carrying out essential repairs to the furniture and plenishings; or

(ii) with the consent of the other spouse, on anything relating to the furniture and plenishings.

(6) An order under subsection (3), (4)(*b*) or (5)(*b*) above may require one spouse to make a payment to the other spouse in implementation of the apportionment.

(7) Any application under subsection (3), (4)(*b*) or (5)(*b*) above shall be made within five years of the date on which any payment in respect of such incurred expenditure was made.

(8) Where—

(*a*) the entitled spouse is a tenant of a matrimonial home; and

(*b*) possession thereof is necessary in order to continue the tenancy; and

(*c*) the entitled spouse abandons such possession,

the tenancy shall be continued by such possession by the non-entitled spouse.

(9) In this section "improvements" includes alterations and enlargement.

NOTE

[1] Applied by the Family Law (Scotland) Act 1985, s. 14(5) (*prosp.*).

Regulation by court of rights of occupancy of matrimonial home

3.—(1) Where there is an entitled and a non-entitled spouse, or where both spouses are entitled, or permitted by a third party, to occupy a matrimonial home, either spouse may apply to the court for an order—

(*a*) declaring the occupancy rights of the applicant spouse;

(*b*) enforcing the occupancy rights of the applicant spouse;

(*c*) restricting the occupancy rights of the non-applicant spouse;

(*d*) regulating the exercise by either spouse of his or her occupancy rights;

(*e*) protecting the occupancy rights of the applicant spouse in relation to the other spouse.

(2) Where one spouse owns or hires, or is acquiring under a hire-purchase or conditional sale agreement, furniture and plenishings in a matrimonial home, the other spouse, if he or she has occupancy rights in that home, may apply to the court for an order granting to the applicant the possession or use in the matrimonial home of any such furniture and plenishings; but, subject to section 2 of this Act, an order under this subsection shall not prejudice the rights of any third party in relation to the non-performance of any obligation under such hire-purchase or conditional sale agreement.

(3) The court shall grant an application under subsection (1)(*a*) above if it appears to the court that the application relates to a matrimonial home; and, on an application under any of paragraphs (*b*) to (*e*) of subsection (1) or under subsection (2) above, the court may make such order relating to the application as appears to it to be just and reasonable having regard to all the circumstances of the case including—

(*a*) the conduct of the spouses in relation to each other and otherwise;

(*b*) the respective needs and financial resources of the spouses;

   (*c*)   the needs of any child of the family;

   (*d*)   the extent (if any) to which—

       (i)   the matrimonial home; and

      (ii)   in relation only to an order under subsection (2) above, any item of furniture and plenishings referred to in that subsection,

      is used in connection with a trade, business or profession of either spouse; and

   (*e*)   whether the entitled spouse offers or has offered to make available to the non-entitled spouse any suitable alternative accommodation.

(4) Pending the making of an order under subsection (3) above, the court, on the application of either spouse, may make such interim order as it may consider necessary or expedient in relation to—

   (*a*)   the residence of either spouse in the home to which the application relates;

   (*b*)   the personal effects of either spouse or of any child of the family; or

   (*c*)   the furniture and plenishings:

Provided that an interim order may be made only if the non-applicant spouse has been afforded an opportunity of being heard by or represented before the court.

(5) The court shall not make an order under subsection (3) or (4) above if it appears that the effect of the order would be to exclude the non-applicant spouse from the matrimonial home.

(6) If the court makes an order under subsection (3) or (4) above which requires the delivery to one spouse of anything which has been left in or removed from the matrimonial home, it may also grant a warrant authorising a messenger-at-arms or sheriff officer to enter the matrimonial home or other premises occupied by the other spouse and to search for and take possession of the thing required to be delivered, if need be by opening shut and lockfast places, and to deliver the thing in accordance with the said order:

Provided that a warrant granted under this subsection shall be executed only after expiry of the period of a charge, being such period as the court shall specify in the order for delivery.

(7) Where it appears to the court—

   (*a*)   on the application of a non-entitled spouse, that that spouse has suffered a loss of occupancy rights or that the quality of the non-entitled spouse's occupation of a matrimonial home has been impaired; or

   (*b*)   on the application of a spouse who has been given the possession or use of furniture and plenishings by virtue of an order under subsection (3) above, that the applicant has suffered a loss of such possession or use or that the quality of the applicant's possession or use of the furniture and plenishings has been impaired,

in consequence of any act or default on the part of the other spouse which was intended to result in such loss or impairment, it may order that other spouse to pay to the applicant such compensation as the court in the circumstances considers just and reasonable in respect of that loss or impairment.

(8) A spouse may renounce in writing the right to apply under subsection (2) above for the possession or use of any item of furniture and plenishings.

Protection of occupancy rights of one spouse against the other

Exclusion orders

4.—[1] (1) Where there is an entitled and a non-entitled spouse, or where both spouses are entitled, or permitted by a third party, to occupy a matrimonial home, either spouse, whether or not that spouse is in occupation at the time of the application, may apply to the court for an order (in this Act referred to as "an exclusion order") suspending the occupancy rights of the other spouse ("the non-applicant spouse") in a matrimonial home.

(2) Subject to subsection (3) below, the court shall make an exclusion order if it appears to the court that the making of the order is necessary for the protection of the applicant or any child of the family from any conduct or threatened or reasonably apprehended conduct of the non-applicant spouse which is or would be injurious to the physical or mental health of the applicant or child.

(3) The court shall not make an exclusion order if it appears to the court that the making of the order would be unjustified or unreasonable—

(a)   having regard to all the circumstances of the case including the matters specified in paragraphs (a) to (e) of section 3(3) of this Act; and

(b)   where the matrimonial home—

    (i)   is or is part of an agricultural holding within the meaning of section 1 of the Agricultural Holdings (Scotland) Act 1949; or

    (ii)   is let, or is a home in respect of which possession is given, to the non-applicant spouse or to both spouses by an employer as an incident of employment,

    subject to a requirement that the non-applicant spouse or, as the case may be, both spouses must reside in the matrimonial home, having regard to that requirement and the likely consequences of the exclusion of the non-applicant spouse from the matrimonial home.

(4) In making an exclusion order the court shall, on the application of the applicant spouse,—

(a)   grant a warrant for the summary ejection of the non-applicant spouse from the matrimonial home;

(b)   grant an interdict prohibiting the non-applicant spouse from entering the matrimonial home without the express permission of the applicant;

(c)   grant an interdict prohibiting the removal by the non-applicant spouse, except with the written consent of the applicant or by a further order of the court, of any furniture and plenishings in the matrimonial home;

unless, in relation to paragraph (a) or (c) above, the non-applicant spouse satisfies the court that it is unnecessary for it to grant such a remedy.

(5) In making an exclusion order the court may—

(a)   grant an interdict prohibiting the non-applicant spouse from entering or remaining in a specified area in the vicinity of the matrimonial home;

(b)   where the warrant for the summary ejection of the non-applicant spouse has been granted in his or her absence, give directions as to the preservation of the non-applicant spouse's goods and effects which remain in the matrimonial home;

(c)   on the application of either spouse, make the exclusion order or the warrant or interdict mentioned in paragraph (a), (b) or (c) of subsection (4) above or paragraph (a) of this subsection subject to such

terms and conditions as the court may prescribe;
(*d*) on application as aforesaid, make such other order as it may consider necessary for the proper enforcement of an order made under subsection (4) above or paragraph (*a*), (*b*) or (*c*) of this subsection.

(6) Pending the making of an exclusion order, the court may, on the application of the applicant spouse, make an interim order suspending the occupancy rights of the non-applicant spouse in the matrimonial home to which the application for the exclusion order relates; and subsections (4) and (5) above shall apply to such interim order as they apply to an exclusion order:

Provided that an interim order may be made only if the non-applicant spouse has been afforded an opportunity of being heard by or represented before the court.

(7) Without prejudice to subsections (1) and (6) above, where both spouses are entitled, or permitted by a third party, to occupy a matrimonial home, it shall be incompetent for one spouse to bring an action of ejection from the matrimonial home against the other spouse.

NOTE
1 As amended by the Law Reform (Miscellaneous Provisions) (Scotland) Act 1985, s. 13(5).

Duration of orders under sections 3 and 4

5.—(1) The court may, on the application of either spouse, vary or recall any order made by it under section 3 or 4 of this Act, but, subject to subsection (2) below, any such order shall, unless previously so varied or recalled, cease to have effect—
(*a*) on the termination of the marriage; or
(*b*) subject to section 6(1) of this Act, where there is an entitled and a non-entitled spouse, on the entitled spouse ceasing to be an entitled spouse in respect of the matrimonial home to which the order relates; or
(*c*) where both spouses are entitled, or permitted by a third party, to occupy the matrimonial home, on both spouses ceasing to be so entitled or permitted.

(2) Without prejudice to the generality of subsection (1) above, an order under section 3(3) or (4) of this Act which grants the possession or use of furniture and plenishings shall cease to have effect if the furniture and plenishings cease to be permitted by a third party to be retained in the matrimonial home.

Occupancy rights in relation to dealings with third parties

Continued exercise of occupancy rights after dealing

6.—(1) Subject to subsection (3) below—
(*a*) the continued exercise of the rights conferred on a non-entitled spouse by the provisions of this Act in respect of a matrimonial home shall not be prejudiced by reason only of any dealing of the entitled spouse relating to that home; and
(*b*) a third party shall not by reason only of such a dealing be entitled to occupy that matrimonial home or any part of it.

(2) In this section and section 7 of this Act—
"dealing" includes the grant of a heritable security and the creation of a trust but does not include a conveyance under section 80 of the

Lands Clauses Consolidation (Scotland) Act 1845;

"entitled spouse" does not include a spouse who, apart from the provisions of this Act—

(a) is permitted by a third party to occupy a matrimonial home; or

(b) is entitled to occupy a matrimonial home along with an individual who is not the other spouse, whether or not that individual has waived his or her right of occupation in favour of the spouse so entitled;

and "non-entitled spouse" shall be construed accordingly.

(3) This section shall not apply in any case where—

(a) the non-entitled spouse in writing either—

    (i) consents or has consented to the dealing, and any consent shall be in such form as the Secretary of State may, by regulations made by statutory instrument, prescribe[1]; or

    (ii) renounces or has renounced his or her occupancy rights in relation to the matrimonial home or property to which the dealing relates;

(b) the court has made an order under section 7 of this Act dispensing with the consent of the non-entitled spouse to the dealing;

(c) the dealing occurred, or implements, a binding obligation entered into by the entitled spouse before his or her marriage to the non-entitled spouse;

(d) the dealing occurred, or implements, a binding obligation entered into before the commencement of this Act;

[2] (e) the dealing comprises a sale to a third party who has acted in good faith, if, at or before the time of the dealing, there is produced to the third party by the seller—

    (i) an affidavit sworn or affirmed by the seller declaring that the subjects of sale are not a matrimonial home in relation to which a spouse of the seller has occupancy rights; or

    (ii) a renunciation of occupancy rights or consent to the dealing which bears to have been properly made or given by the non-entitled spouse.

For the purposes of this paragraph, the time of the dealing, in the case of the sale of an interest in heritable property, is the date of delivery to the purchaser of the deed transferring title to that interest; or

(f) the entitled spouse has permanently ceased to be entitled to occupy the matrimonial home, and at any time thereafter a continuous period of five years has elapsed during which the non-entitled spouse has not occupied the matrimonial home.

(4) The Land Registration (Scotland) Act 1979 shall be amended as follows—

(a) in section 6(4)—

(i) after the words "the interest of" there shall be inserted "(i)"; and

(ii) after the words "is not a long lease" there shall be inserted—

    "and

    (ii) a non-entitled spouse within the meaning of section 6 of the Matrimonial Homes (Family Protection) (Scotland) Act 1981.";

(*b*) in paragraph (*b*) of section 9(4)—

    (i) after the words "the interest of" these shall be inserted "(i)"; and

    (ii) after the words "is not a long lease" there shall be inserted—

    "and

      (ii) a non-entitled spouse within the meaning of section 6 of the Matrimonial Homes (Family Protection) (Scotland) Act 1981."; and

(*c*) in section 28 in the definition of overriding interest after paragraph (*g*) there shall be inserted the following—

    "(*gg*) the non-entitled spouse within the meaning of section 6 of the Matrimonial Homes (Family Protection) (Scotland) Act 1981;".

NOTES

[1] See S.I. 1982 No. 971, and Appendix III.

[2] As amended by the Law Reform (Miscellaneous Provisions) (Scotland) Act 1985, s. 13(6). By s. 13(11) of the same Act: "Any—

(*a*) affidavit lawfully sworn or affirmed before the commencement of this section in pursuance of paragraph (*e*) of subsection (3) of section 6 or subsection (2) of section 8 of that Act;

(*b*) consent lawfully given before such commencement in pursuance of the said subsection (2),

shall have effect for the purposes of the said subsection (3) as amended by this section or, as the case may be, section 8(2A) of that Act as if it had been duly sworn, affirmed or, as the case may be, given in pursuance of the said paragraph (*e*) as so amended or, as the case may be, the said section 8(2A)."

Dispensation by court with spouse's consent to dealing

7.—(1) The court may, on the application of an entitled spouse or any other person having an interest, make an order dispensing with the consent of a non-entitled spouse to a dealing which has taken place or a proposed dealing, if—

(*a*) such consent is unreasonably withheld;

(*b*) such consent cannot be given by reason of physical or mental disability;

(*c*) the non-entitled spouse cannot be found after reasonable steps have been taken to trace him or her; or

(*d*) the non-entitled spouse is a minor.

(2) For the purposes of subsection (1)(*a*) above, a non-entitled spouse shall have unreasonably withheld consent to a dealing which has taken place or a proposed dealing, where it appears to the court—

(*a*) that the non-entitled spouse has led the entitled spouse to believe that he or she would consent to the dealing and that the non-entitled spouse would not be prejudiced by any change in the circumstances of the case since such apparent consent was given; or

(*b*) that the entitled spouse has, having taken all reasonable steps to do so, been unable to obtain an answer to a request for consent.

(3) The court, in considering whether to make an order under subsection (1) above, shall have regard to all the circumstances of the case including the matters specified in paragraphs (*a*) to (*e*) of section 3(3) of this Act.

(4) Where—

(*a*) an application is made for an order under this section; and

(*b*) an action is or has been raised by a non-entitled spouse to enforce occupancy rights,

the action shall be sisted until the conclusion of the proceedings on the application.

(5) [Repealed (*prosp.*) by the Family Law (Scotland) Act 1985, Sched. 2.]

Interests of heritable creditors

8.—(1) The rights of a third party with an interest in the matrimonial home as a creditor under a secured loan in relation to the non-performance of any obligation under the loan shall not be prejudiced by reason only of the occupancy rights of the non-entitled spouse; but where a non-entitled spouse has or obtains occupation of a matrimonial home and—

(*a*)   the entitled spouse is not in occupation; and

(*b*)   there is a third party with such an interest in the matrimonial home, the court may on the application of the third party, make an order requiring the non-entitled spouse to make any payment due by the entitled spouse in respect of the loan.

[1] (2) This section shall not apply to secured loans in respect of which the security was granted prior to the commencement of section 13 of the Law Reform (Miscellaneous Provisions) (Scotland) Act 1985 unless the third party in granting the secured loan acted in good faith and before the granting of the loan there was produced to the third party by the entitled spouse—

(*a*)   an affidavit sworn or affirmed by the entitled spouse declaring that there is no non-entitled spouse; or

(*b*)   a renunciation of occupancy rights or consent to the taking of the loan which bears to have been properly made or given by the non-entitled spouse.

[2] (2B) For the purposes of subsections (2) and (2A) above, the time of security was granted after the commencement of section 13 of the Law Reform (Miscellaneous Provisions) (Scotland) Act 1985 unless the third party in granting the secured loan acted in good faith and at or before the granting of the security there was produced to the third party by the grantor—

(*a*)   an affidavit sworn or affirmed by the grantor declaring that the security subjects are not a matrimonial home in relation to which a spouse of the grantor has occupancy rights; or

(*b*)   a renunciation of occupancy rights or consent to the granting of the security which bears to have been properly made or given by the non-entitled spouse.

[2] (2B) For the purposes of subsection (2) and (2A) above, the time of granting a security, in the case of a heritable security, is the date of delivery of the deed creating the security.

NOTES

[1] As amended by the Law Reform (Miscellaneous Provisions) (Scotland) Act 1985, s. 13(7), with effect from 30th December 1985. By section 13(11) of the same Act: "Any—

(*a*)   affidavits lawfully sworn or affirmed before the commencement of this section in pursuance of paragraph (*e*) of subsection (3) of section 6 or subsection (2) of section 8 of that Act;

(*b*)   consent lawfully given before such commencement in pursuance of the said subsection (2),

shall have effect for the purposes of the said subsection (3) as amended by this section or, as the case may be, section 8(2A) of that Act as if it had been duly sworn, affirmed or, as the case may be, given in pursuance of the said paragraph (*e*) as so amended or, as the case may be, the said section 8(2A)."

[2] Inserted by the Law Reform (Miscellaneous Provisions) (Scotland) Act 1985, s. 13(8), with effect from 30th December 1985.

Provisions where both spouses have title

9.—(1) Subject to subsection (2) below, where, apart from the provisions of this Act, both spouses are entitled to occupy a matrimonial home—

(*a*) the rights in that home of one spouse shall not be prejudiced by reason only of any dealing of the other spouse; and

(*b*) a third party shall not by reason only of such a dealing be entitled to occupy that matrimonial home or any part of it.

(2) The definition of "dealing" in section 6(2) of this Act and sections 6(3) and 7 of this Act shall apply for the purposes of subsection (1) above as they apply for the purposes of section 6(1) of this Act subject to the following modifications—

(*a*) any reference to the entitled spouse and to the non-entitled spouse shall be construed as a reference to a spouse who has entered into, or as the case may be, proposes to enter into a dealing and to the other spouse respectively; and

(*b*) in paragraph (*b*) of section 7(4) the reference to occupancy rights shall be construed as a reference to any rights in the matrimonial home.

Protection of rights of spouse against arrangements intended to defeat them

10. [Repealed by the Bankruptcy (Scotland) Act 1985, Sched. 8.]

Poinding

[1] **11.**—Where a poinding has been executed of furniture and plenishings of which the debtor's spouse has the possession or use by virtue of an order under section 3(3) or (4) of this Act, the sheriff, on the application of that spouse within 40 days of the date of execution of the poinding, may—

(*a*) declare that the poinding is null; or

(*b*) make such order as he thinks appropriate to protect such possession or use by that spouse,

if he is satisfied that the purpose of the diligence was wholly or mainly to prevent such possession or use.

NOTE

[1] Applied by the Family Law (Scotland) Act 1985, s. 14(5) (*prosp.*).

Adjudication

[1] **12.**—(1) Where a matrimonial home of which there is an entitled spouse and a non-entitled spouse is adjudged, the Court of Session, on the application of the non-entitled spouse within 40 days of the date of the decree of adjudication, may—

(*a*) order the reduction of the decree; or

(*b*) make such order as it thinks appropriate to protect the occupancy rights of the non-entitled spouse,

if it is satisfied that the purpose of the diligence was wholly or mainly to defeat the occupancy rights of the non-entitled spouse.

(2) In this section, "entitled spouse" and "non-entitled spouse" have the same meanings respectively as in section 6(2) of this Act.

NOTE

[1] Applied by the Family Law (Scotland) Act 1985, s. 14(5) (*prosp.*).

Transfer of tenancy

13.—(1) The court may, on the application of a non-entitled spouse, make an order transferring the tenancy of a matrimonial home to that spouse and providing, subject to subsection (11) below, for the payment by the non-entitled spouse to the entitled spouse of such compensation as seems just and reasonable in all the circumstances of the case.

¹ (2) In an action—

(*a*) for divorce, the Court of Session or a sheriff;

(*b*) for nullity of marriage, the Court of Session,

may, on granting decree or within such period as the court may specify on granting decree, make an order granting an application under subsection (1) above.

(3) In determining whether to grant an application under subsection (1) above, the court shall have regard to all the circumstances of the case including the matters specified in paragraphs (*a*) to (*e*) of section 3(3) of this Act and the suitability of the applicant to become the tenant and the applicant's capacity to perform the obligations under the lease of the matrimonial home.

(4) The non-entitled spouse shall serve a copy of an application under subsection (1) above on the landlord and, before making an order under subsection (1) above, the court shall give the landlord an opportunity of being heard by it.

(5) On the making of an order granting an application under subsection (1) above, the tenancy shall vest in the non-entitled spouse without intimation to the landlord, subject to all the liabilities under the lease (other than any arrears of rent for the period before the making of the order, which shall remain the liability of the original entitled spouse).

(6) The clerk of court shall notify the landlord of the making of an order granting an application under subsection (1) above.

(7) It shall not be competent for a non-entitled spouse to apply for an order under subsection (1) above where the matrimonial home—

(*a*)   is let to the entitled spouse by his or her employer as an incident of employment, and the lease is subject to a requirement that the entitled spouse must reside therein;

(*b*)   is or is part of an agricultural holding;

(*c*)   is on or pertains to a croft or the subject of a cottar or the holding of a landholder or a statutory small tenant;

(*d*)   is let on a long lease;

(*e*)   is part of the tenancy land of a tenant-at-will.

(8) In subsection (6) above—

"agricultural holding" has the same meaning as in section 1 of the Agricultural Holdings (Scotland) Act 1949;

"cottar" has the same meaning as in section 28(4) of the Crofters (Scotland) Act 1955;

"croft" has the same meaning as in the Crofters (Scotland) Act 1955;

"holding", in relation to a landholder and a statutory small tenant, "landholder" and "statutory small tenant" have the same meanings respectively as in sections 2(1), 2(2) and 32(1) of the Small Landholders (Scotland) Act 1911;

"long lease" has the same meaning as in section 28(1) of the Land Registration (Scotland) Act 1979;

"tenant-at-will" has the same meaning as in section 20(8) of the Land Registration (Scotland) Act 1979.

(9) Where both spouses are joint or common tenants of a matrimonial home, the court may, on the application of one of the spouses, make an order vesting the tenancy in that spouse solely and providing, subject to subsection (11) below, for the payment by the applicant to the other spouse of such compensation as seems just and reasonable in the circumstances of the case.

(10) Subsections (2) to (8) above shall apply for the purposes of an order under subsection (9) above as they apply for the purposes of an order under subsection (1) above subject to the following modifications—

(a) in subsection (3) for the word "tenant" there shall be substituted the words "sole tenant";

(b) in subsection (4) for the words "non-entitled" there should be substituted the word "applicant";

(c) in subsection (5) for the words "non-entitled" and "liability of the original entitled spouse" there shall be substituted respectively the words "applicant" and "joint and several liability of both spouses";

(d) in subsection (7)—

(i) for the words "a non-entitled" there shall be substituted the words "an applicant";

(ii) for paragraph (a) there shall be substituted the following paragraph—

"(a) is let to both spouses by their employer as an incident of employment, and the lease is subject to a requirement that both spouses must reside there;";

(iii) paragraphs (c) and (e) shall be omitted.

(11) Where the matrimonial home is a secure tenancy within the meaning of the Tenants' Rights, Etc. (Scotland) Act 1980, no account shall be taken, in assessing the amount of any compensation to be awarded under subsection (1) or (9) above, of the loss, by virtue of the transfer of the tenancy of the home, of a right to purchase the home under Part I of that Act.

(12) In the Tenants' Rights, Etc. (Scotland) Act 1980—

(a) paragraph 6 of Part I of Schedule 2 is repealed.

(b) [Repealed by the Tenants' Rights, Etc. (Scotland) Amendment Act 1984, s. 8(2) and Sched.]

NOTE

[1] As amended (*prosp.*) by the Family Law (Scotland) Act 1985, Sched. 1, para.11.

Matrimonial interdicts

Interdict competent where spouses live together

14.—(1) It shall not be incompetent for the court to entertain an application by a spouse for a matrimonial interdict by reason only that the spouses are living together as man and wife.

(2) In this section and section 15 of this Act—

"matrimonial interdict" means an interdict including an interim interdict which—

(a) restrains or prohibits any conduct of one spouse towards the other spouse or a child of the family, or

(b) prohibits a spouse from entering or remaining in a matrimonial home or in a specified area in the vicinity of the matrimonial home.

Attachment of powers of arrest to matrimonial interdicts

15.—(1) The court shall, on the application of the applicant spouse, attach a power of arrest—

(a) to any matrimonial interdict which is ancillary to an exclusion order, including an interim order under section 4(6) of this Act;

(b) to any other matrimonial interdict where the non-applicant spouse has had the opportunity of being heard by or represented before the court, unless it appears to the court that in all the circumstances of the case such a power is unnecessary.

(2) A power of arrest attached to an interdict by virtue of subsection (1) above shall not have effect until such interdict is served on the non-applicant spouse, and such a power of arrest shall, unless previously recalled, cease to have effect upon the termination of the marriage.

(3) If, by virtue of subsection (1) above, a power of arrest is attached to an interdict, a constable may arrest without warrant the non-applicant spouse if he has reasonable cause for suspecting that spouse of being in breach of the interdict.

(4) If, by virtue of subsection (1) above, a power of arrest is attached to an interdict, the applicant spouse shall, as soon as possible after service of the interdict on the non-applicant spouse, ensure that there is delivered—

(a) to the chief constable of the police area in which the matrimonial home is situated; and

(b) if the applicant spouse resides in another police area, to the chief constable of that other police area,

a copy of the application for the interdict and of the interlocutor granting the interdict together with a certificate of service of the interdict.

(5) Where any matrimonial interdict to which, by virtue of subsection (1) above there is attached a power of arrest, is varied or recalled, the spouse who applied for the variation or recall shall ensure that there is delivered—

(a) to the chief constable of the police area in which the matrimonial home is situated; and

(b) if the applicant spouse (within the meaning of subsection (6) below) resides in another police area, to the chief constable of that other police area,

a copy of the application for variation or recall and of the interlocutor granting the variation or recall.

(6) In this section and in sections 16 and 17 of this Act—

"applicant spouse" means the spouse who has applied for the interdict; and

"non-applicant spouse" shall be construed accordingly.

Police powers after arrest

16.—(1) Where a person has been arrested under section 15(3) of this Act, the officer in charge of a police station may—

(a) if satisfied that there is no likelihood of violence to the applicant spouse or any child of the family, liberate that person unconditionally; or

(b) refuse to liberate that person; and such refusal and the detention of that person until his or her appearance in court by virtue of—

(i)   section 17(2) of this Act; or

(ii) any provision of the Criminal Procedure (Scotland) Act 1975, shall not subject the officer to any claim whatsoever.

(2) Where a person arrested under section 15(3) of this Act is liberated under subsection (1) above, the facts and circumstances which gave rise to the arrest shall be reported forthwith to the procurator fiscal who, if he decides to take no criminal proceedings in respect of those facts and circumstances, shall at the earliest opportunity take all reasonable steps to intimate his decision to the persons mentioned in paragraphs (a) and (b) of section 17(4) of this Act.

Procedure after arrest

17.—(1) The provisions of this section shall apply only where—
- (a) the non-applicant spouse has not been liberated under section 16(1) of this Act; and
- (b) the procurator fiscal decides that no criminal proceedings are to be taken in respect of the facts and circumstances which gave rise to the arrest.

(2) The non-applicant spouse who has been arrested under section 15(3) of this Act shall wherever practicable be brought before the sheriff sitting as a court of summary criminal jurisdiction for the district in which he or she was arrested not later than in the course of the first day after the arrest, such day not being a Saturday, a Sunday or a court holiday prescribed for that court under section 10 of the Bail etc. (Scotland) Act 1980:

Provided that nothing in this subsection shall prevent the non-applicant spouse from being brought before the sheriff on a Saturday, a Sunday or such a court holiday where the sheriff is in pursuance of the said section 10 sitting on such a day for the disposal of criminal business.

(3) Subsections (1) and (2) of section 3 of the Criminal Justice (Scotland) Act 1980 (intimation to a named person) shall apply to a non-applicant spouse who has been arrested under section 15(3) of this Act as they apply to a person who has been arrested in respect of any offence.

(4) The procurator fiscal shall at the earliest opportunity, and in any event prior to the non-applicant spouse being brought before the sheriff under subsection (2) above, take all reasonable steps to intimate—
- (a) to the applicant spouse; and
- (b) to the solicitor who acted for that spouse when the interdict was granted or to any other solicitor who the procurator fiscal has reason to believe acts for the time being for that spouse,

that the criminal proceedings referred to in subsection (1) above will not be taken.

(5) On the non-applicant spouse being brought before the sheriff under subsection (2) above, the following procedure shall apply—
- (a) the procurator fiscal shall present to the court a petition containing—
  - (i) a statement of the particulars of the non-applicant spouse;
  - (ii) a statement of the facts and circumstances which gave rise to the arrest; and
  - (iii) a request that the non-applicant spouse be detained for a further period not exceeding two days;
- (b) if it appears to the sheriff that—
  - (i) the statement referred to in paragraph (a)(ii) above discloses a *prima facie* breach of interdict by the non-applicant spouse;
  - (ii) proceedings for breach of interdict will be taken; and
  - (iii) there is a substantial risk of violence by the non-applicant spouse against the applicant spouse or any child of the family,

he may order the non-applicant spouse to be detained for a further period not exceeding two days;

(c) in any case to which paragraph (b) above does not apply, the non-applicant spouse shall, unless in custody in respect of any other matter, be released from custody;

and in computing the period of two days referred to in paragraphs (a) and (b) above, no account shall be taken of a Saturday or Sunday or of any holiday in the court in which the proceedings for breach of interdict will require to be raised.

Cohabiting couples

Occupancy rights of cohabiting couples

18.—[1] (1) If a man and a woman are living with each other as if they were man and wife ("a cohabiting couple") in a house which, apart from the provisions of this section—

(a) one of them (an "entitled partner") is entitled, or permitted by a third party, to occupy; and

(b) the other (a "non-entitled partner") is not so entitled or permitted to occupy,

the court may, on the application of the non-entitled partner, if it appears that the man and the woman are a cohabiting couple in that house, grant occupancy rights therein to the applicant for such period, not exceeding six months, as the court may specify:

Provided that the court may extend the said period for a further period or periods, no such period exceeding six months.

(2) In determining whether for the purpose of subsection (1) above a man and woman are a cohabiting couple the court shall have regard to all the circumstances of the case including—

(a) the time for which it appears they have been living together; and

(b) whether there are any children of the relationship.

(3) While an order granting an application under subsection (1) above or an extension of such an order is in force, or where both partners of a cohabiting couple are entitled, or permitted by a third party, to occupy the house where they are cohabiting, the following provisions of this Act shall subject to any necessary modifications—

(a) apply to the cohabiting couple as they apply to parties to a marriage; and

(b) have effect in relation to any child residing with the cohabiting couple as they have effect in relation to a child of the family,

section 2;

section 3, except subsection (1)(a);

section 4;

in section 5(1), the words from the beginning to "Act" where it first occurs;

sections 13 and 14;

section 15, except the words in subsection (2) from "and such a power of arrest" to the end;

sections 16 and 17;

and

section 22,

and any reference in these provisions to a matrimonial home shall be construed as a reference to a house.

(4) Any order under section 3 or 4 of this Act as applied to a cohabiting couple by subsection (3) above shall have effect—

(*a*) if one of them is a non-entitled partner, for such a period, not exceeding the period or periods which from time to time may be specified in any order under subsection (1) above for which occupancy rights have been granted under that subsection, as may be specified in the order;

(*b*) if they are both entitled, or permitted by a third party, to occupy the house, until a further order of the court.

(5) Nothing in this section shall prejudice the rights of any third party having an interest in the house referred to in subsection (1) above.

¹ (6) In this section—

"house" includes a caravan, houseboat or other structure in which the couple are cohabiting and any garden or other ground or building attached to, and usually occupied with, or otherwise required for the amenity or convenience of, the house, caravan, houseboat or other structure;

"occupancy rights" means the following rights of a non-entitled partner—

(*a*) if in occupation, a right to continue to occupy the house;

(*b*) if not in occupation, a right to enter into and occupy the house;

and, without prejudice to the generality of these rights, includes the right to continue to occupy or, as the case may be, to enter and occupy the house together with any child residing with the cohabiting couple;

"entitled partner" includes a partner who is entitled, or permitted by a third party, to occupy the house along with an individual who is not the other partner only if that individual has waived his or her right of occupation in favour of the partner so entitled or permitted.

NOTE
¹ As amended by the Law Reform (Miscellaneous Provisions) (Scotland) Act 1985, s. 13(9).

Miscellaneous and General

Rights of occupancy in relation to division and sale

19. Where a spouse brings an action for the division and sale of a matrimonial home which the spouses own in common, the court, after having regard to all the circumstances of the case including—

(*a*) the matters specified in paragraphs (*a*) to (*d*) of section 3(3) of this Act; and

(*b*) whether the spouse bringing the action offers or has offered to make available to the other spouse any suitable alternative accommodation,

may refuse to grant decree in that action or may postpone the granting of decree for such period as it may consider reasonable in the circumstances or may grant decree subject to such conditions as it may prescribe.

Spouse's consent in relation to calling up of standard securities over matrimonial homes

20. Section 19(10) of the Conveyancing and Feudal Reform (Scotland) Act 1970 shall have effect as if at the end there were added the following proviso—

"Provided that, without prejudice to the foregoing generality, if the standard security is over a matrimonial home as defined in section 22 of the Matrimonial Homes (Family Protection) (Scotland) Act 1981, the spouse on whom the calling-up notice has been served may not dispense with or shorten the said period without the consent in writing of the other spouse.".

Procedural provision

21. Section 2(2) of the Law Reform (Husband and Wife) Act 1962 (dismissal by court of delictual proceedings between spouses) shall not apply to any proceedings brought before the court in pursuance of any provision of this Act.

Interpretation

[1] **22.** In this Act—

"caravan" means a caravan which is mobile or affixed to the land;

"child of the family" includes any child or grandchild of either spouse, and any person who has been brought up or accepted by either spouse as if he or she were a child of that spouse, whatever the age of such a child, grandchild or person may be;

"the court" means the Court of Session or the sheriff;

"furniture and plenishings" means any article situated in a matrimonial home which—

(a) is owned or hired by either spouse or is being acquired by either spouse under a hire-purchase agreement or conditional sale agreement; and

(b) is reasonably necessary to enable the home to be used as a family residence,

but does not include any vehicle, caravan or houseboat, or such other structure as is mentioned in the definition of "matrimonial home";

"matrimonial home" means any house, caravan, houseboat or other structure which has been provided or has been made available by one or both of the spouses as, or has become, a family residence and includes any garden or other ground or building attached to, and usually occupied with, or otherwise required for the amenity or convenience of, the house, caravan, houseboat or other structure but does not include a residence provided or made available by one spouse for that spouse to reside in, whether with any child of the family or not, separately from the other spouse;

"occupancy rights" has, subject to section 18(6) of this Act, the meaning assigned by section 1(4) of this Act;

"the sheriff" includes the sheriff having jurisdiction in the district where the matrimonial home is situated;

[2] "tenant" includes sub-tenant and a statutory tenant as defined in section 3 of the Rent (Scotland) Act 1984 and "tenancy" shall be construed accordingly;

"entitled spouse" and "non-entitled spouse", subject to sections 6(2) and 12(2) of this Act, have the meanings respectively assigned to them by section 1 of this Act.

NOTE

[1] As amended by the Law Reform (Miscellaneous Provisions) (Scotland) Act 1985, s. 13(10).

2 See the Rent (Scotland) Act 1984, Sched. 8, Pt. I, para. 2.

Short title, commencement and extent

23.—(1) This Act may be cited as the Matrimonial Homes (Family Protection) (Scotland) Act 1981.

¹ (2) This Act (except this section) shall come into operation on such day as the Secretary of State may by order made by statutory instrument appoint, and different days may be so appointed for different provisions and for different purposes.

(3) This Act extends to Scotland only.

NOTE

¹ 1st September 1982 for the whole Act: S.I. 1982 No. 972.

Small Landholders (Scotland) Act 1911

Who to be landholders

2. —(1) In the Crofters Acts and this Act (herein-after referred to collectively as the Landholders Acts) the word "holding" means and includes—

(i) As from the commencement of this Act, every holding which at the commencement of this Act is held by a crofter to whom in respect of such holding the Act of 1886 applies (herein-after referred to as an existing crofter);

(ii) As from the commencement of this Act, and subject as herein-after provided, every holding which at the commencement of this Act is held by a tenant from year to year who resides on or within three kilometres from the holding, and by himself or his family cultivates the holding with or without hired labour (herein-after referred to as an existing yearly tenant);

(iii) As from the termination of the lease, and subject as herein-after provided, every holding which at the commencement of this Act is held under a lease for a term longer than one year by a tenant who resides on or within three kilometres from the holding, and by himself or his family cultivates the holding with or without hired labour (such tenant, or his heir or successor, as the case may be, holding under the lease at the termination thereof being herein-after referred to as a qualified leaseholder):

Provided that such tenant from year to year or leaseholder—

(*a*) shall (unless disqualified under section 26 of this Act) be held an existing yearly tenant or a qualified leaseholder within the meaning of this section in every case where it is agreed between the landlord and tenant or leaseholder, or in the event of dispute, proved to the satisfaction of the Land Court, that such tenant or leaseholder or his predecessor in the same family has provided or paid for the whole or the greater part of the buildings or other permanent improvements on the holding without receiving from the landlord or any predecessor in title payment or fair consideration therefor; and

(*b*) in every other case shall not be held an existing yearly tenant or a qualified leaseholder within the meaning of this section, but shall (unless disqualified under section 26 of this Act) in respect of the holding be subject to the provisions of this Act regarding statutory small tenants;

(iv) As from the date of registration, every holding which is constituted by the registration of an applicant in respect thereof on his application under the provisions of this Act respecting the constitution of new holdings (herein-after referred to as a new holder).

(2) In the Landholders Acts the word "landholder" means and includes, as from the respective dates above mentioned, every existing crofter, every existing yearly tenant, every qualified leaseholder, and every new holder, and

the successors of every such person in the holding being his heirs or legatees.

Provisions as to statutory small tenants

32.—(1) A statutory small tenant means and includes a tenant from year to year, or leaseholder, not otherwise disqualified in terms of this Act, in regard to whom section 2 of this Act provides that he shall not be held an existing yearly tenant or a qualified leaseholder, and the successors of such tenant or leaseholder in the holding, being his heirs, legatees (if within the relationship specified in section 16 of the Act of 1886), or assignees (if assignation be permitted by the lease) . . .

Agricultural Holdings (Scotland) Act 1949

Meaning of "agricultural holding"

1.—(1) In this Act the expression "agricultural holding" means the aggregate of the agricultural land comprised in a lease, not being a lease under which the said land is let to the tenant during his continuance in any office, appointment or employment held under the landlord.

(2) For the purposes of this and the next following section, the expression "agricultural land" means land used for agriculture which is so used for the purposes of a trade or business, and includes any other land which, by virtue of a designation of the Secretary of State under subsection (1) of section 86 of the Agriculture (Scotland) Act, 1948, is agricultural land within the meaning of that Act.

Crofters (Scotland) Act 1955

Definition of "croft" and "crofter", and conditions of tenure of crofter

3.—(1) In this Act the expression "croft" means—

(*a*) as from the commencement of this Act, every holding (whether occupied by a landholder or not) situate in the crofting counties which was, immediately before the commencement of this Act, a holding to which any of the provisions of the Landholders Acts relating to landholders applied;

(*b*) as from the commencement of this Act, every holding situate as aforesaid which was, immediately before the commencement of this Act, a holding to which the provisions of the Landholders Acts relating to statutory small tenants applied;

(*c*) as from the date of registration, every holding situate as aforesaid which was before the commencement of the Crofters (Scotland) Act 1961, constituted a croft by the registration of the tenant thereof as a crofter under section four of this Act;

(*d*) as from the date of the direction, every holding situated as aforesaid as to which the Secretary of State has directed under subsection (1) of section 2 of the Crofters (Scotland) Act 1961, that it shall be a croft.

Provisions as to cottars

28.— . . .(4)

"cottar" means the occupier of a dwelling-house situate in the crofting counties with or without land who pays no rent, or the tenant from year to year of a dwelling-house situate as aforesaid who resides therein and who pays therefor an annual rent not exceeding six pounds in money, whether with or without garden ground but without arable or pasture land.

Law Reform (Husband and Wife) Act 1962

Proceedings as between husband and wife in respect of delict

2.—(1) Subject to the provisions of this section, each of the parties to a marriage shall have the like right to bring proceedings against the other in respect of a wrongful or negligent act or omission, or for the prevention of a wrongful act, as if they were not married.

(2) Where any such proceedings are brought by one of the parties to a marriage against the other during the subsistence of the marriage, the court may dismiss the proceedings if it appears that no substantial benefit would accrue to either party from the continuation thereof; and it shall be the duty of the court to consider at an early stage of the proceedings whether the power to dismiss the proceedings under this subsection should or should not be exercised.

Conveyancing and Feudal Reform (Scotland) Act 1970

Calling-up of standard security

19.— ... (10) The period of notice mentioned in the calling-up notice may be effectively dispensed with or shortened by the person on whom it is served, with the consent of the creditors, if any, holding securities *pari passu* with, or postponed to, the security held by the creditor serving the calling-up notice, by a minute written or endorsed upon the said notice, or a copy thereof, in conformity with Form C of Schedule 6 to this Act.

Land Registration (Scotland) Act 1979

Tenants-at-will

20.— ... (8) In this section and in sections 21 and 22 of this Act, "tenant-at-will" means a person—

(*a*) who, not being—
   (i)   a tenant under a lease;
   (ii) a kindly tenant; or
   (iii) a tenant or occupier by virtue of any enactment,
is by custom and usage the occupier (actual or constructive) of land on which there is a building or buildings erected or acquired for value by him or any predecessor of his;

(*b*) who is under an obligation to pay a ground rent to the owner of the land in respect of the said land but not in respect of the building or buildings on it, or would have been under such an obligation if the ground rent had not been redeemed; and

(*c*) whose right of occupancy of the land is without ish.

Interpretation, etc.

28.—(1)
"long lease" means a probative lease—
(*a*) exceeding 20 years; or

(*b*) which is subject to any provision whereby any person holding the interest of the grantor is under a future obligation, if so requested by the grantee, to renew the lease so that the total duration could (in terms of the lease, as renewed, and without any subsequent agreement, express or implied, between the persons holding the interests of the grantor and the grantee) extend for more than 20 years; ...

Bankruptcy (Scotland) Act 1985

Power of permanent trustee in relation to the debtor's family home

40.—(1) Before the permanent trustee sells or disposes of any right or interest in the debtor's family home he shall—
  (*a*) obtain the relevant consent; or
  (*b*) where he is unable to do so, obtain the authority of the court in accordance with subsection (2) below.

(2) Where the permanent trustee requires to obtain the authority of the court in terms of subsection (1)(*b*) above, the court, after having regard to all the circumstances of the case, including—
  (*a*) the needs and financial resources of the debtor's spouse or former spouse;
  (*b*) the needs and financial resources of any child of the family;
  (*c*) the interests of the creditors;
  (*d*) the length of the period during which (whether before or after the relevant date) the family home was used as a residence by any of the persons referred to in paragraph (*a*) or (*b*) above,
may refuse to grant the application or may postpone the granting of the application for such period (not exceeding 12 months) as it may consider reasonable in the circumstances or may grant the application subject to such conditions as it may prescribe.

(3) Subsection (2) above shall apply—
  (*a*) to an action for division and sale of the debtor's family home; or
  (*b*) to an action for the purpose of obtaining vacant possession of the debtor's family home,
brought by the permanent trustee as it applies to an application under subsection (1)(*b*) above and, for the purposes of this subsection, any reference in the said subsection (2) to that granting of the application shall be construed as a reference to the granting of decree in the action.

(4) In this section—
  (*a*) "family home" means any property in which, at the relevant date, the debtor had (whether alone or in common with any other person) a right or interest, being property which was occupied at that date as a residence by the debtor and his spouse or by the debtor's spouse or former spouse (in any case with or without a child of the family) or by the debtor with a child of the family;
  (*b*) "child of the family" includes any child or grandchild of either the debtor or his spouse or former spouse, and any person who has been brought up or accepted by either the debtor or his spouse or former spouse as if he or she were a child of the debtor, spouse or former spouse whatever the age of such a child, grandchild or person may be;
  (*c*) "relevant consent" means in relation to the sale or disposal of any right or interest in a family home—

> (i) in a case where the family home is occupied by the debtor's spouse or former spouse, the consent of the spouse, or, as the case may be, the former spouse, whether or not the family home is also occupied by the debtor;
>
> (ii) where sub-paragraph (i) above does not apply, in a case where the family home is occupied by the debtor with a child of the family, the consent of the debtor; and

(*d*) "relevant date" means the day immediately preceding the date of sequestration.

Protection of rights of spouse against arrangements intended to defeat them

41.—(1) If a debtor's sequestrated estate includes a matrimonial home of which the debtor, immediately before the date of issue of the act and warrant of the permanent trustee (or, if more than one such act and warrant is issued in the sequestration, of the first such issue) was an entitled spouse and the other spouse is a non-entitled spouse—

(*a*) the permanent trustee shall, where he—

> (i) is aware that the entitled spouse is married to the non-entitled spouse; and
>
> (ii) knows where the non-entitled spouse is residing,

inform the non-entitled spouse, within the period of 14 days beginning with that date, of the fact that sequestration of the entitled spouse's estate has been awarded, of the right of petition which exists under section 16 of this Act and of the effect of paragraph (*b*) below; and

(*b*) the Court of Session, on the petition under section 16 of this Act of the non-entitled spouse presented either within the period of 40 days beginning with that date or within the period of 10 weeks beginning with the date of sequestration may—

> (i) under section 17 of this Act recall the sequestration; or
>
> (ii) make such order as it thinks appropriate to protect the occupancy rights of the non-entitled spouse;

if it is satisfied that the purpose of the petition for sequestration was wholly or mainly to defeat the occupancy rights of the non-entitled spouse.

(2) In subsection (1) above—

"entitled spouse" and "non-entitled spouse" have the same meanings as in section 6 of the Matrimonial Homes (Family Protection) (Scotland) Act 1981;

"matrimonial home" has the meaning assigned by section 22 of that Act as amended by the Law Reform (Miscellaneous Provisions) (Scotland) Act 1985; and

"occupancy rights" has the meaning assigned by section 1(4) of the said Act of 1981.

Criminal Justice (Scotland) Act 1980

Right to have someone informed when arrested or detained

3.—(1) Without prejudice to section 19 or 305 of the 1975 Act (intimation to solicitor following arrest), a person who, not being a person in respect of whose custody or detention subsection (3) below applies[1]—

(*a*) has been arrested and is in custody in a police station or other premises, shall be entitled to have intimation of his custody and of the place where he is being held sent, to a person reasonably named by him;

(*b*) is being detained under section 2 of this Act in a police station or other premises, shall be entitled to have intimation of his detention and of the place where he is being detained sent, to a solicitor and to one other person reasonably named by him,

without delay or, where some delay is necessary in the interest of the investigation or the prevention of crime or the apprehension of offenders, with no more delay than is so necessary; and the person shall be informed of such entitlement—

(i)   on arrival at the police station or other premises; or
(ii) where he is not arrested, or as the case may be detained, until after such arrival, on such arrest or detention.

(2) Where the person mentioned in paragraph (*a*) of subsection (1) above requests such intimation to be sent as is specified in that paragraph there shall be recorded the time when such request is—

(i)   made;
(ii) complied with.

NOTE
[1] Subsection (3) relates to detention of children.

[1] 1. Prescribed Forms of Consent (Section 6(3)(a)(i))

NOTE

[1] Taken from the Matrimonial Homes (Form of Consent) (Scotland) Regulations 1982 (S.I. 1982 No. 971).

(a) Consent to be Inserted in the Deed Effecting the Dealing

(The following words should be inserted where appropriate in the deed. The consenter should sign as a party to the deed.)
... with the consent of A.B. (*designation*), the spouse of the said C.D., for the purposes of the Matrimonial Homes (Family Protection) (Scotland) Act 1981 ... [To be attested]

(b) Consent in a Separate Document

I, A.B. (*designation*), spouse of C.D. (*designation*), hereby consent, for the purposes of the Matrimonial Homes (Family Protection) (Scotland) Act 1981, to the undernoted dealing of the said C.D. relating to (*here describe the matrimonial home or the part of it to which the dealing relates*).

Dealing referred to:—
(Here describe the dealing.)
[To be attested].

2. Style of Affidavit in Connection with Sale (Section 6(3)(e))

I, A [*design*] make oath/do solemnly and sincerely affirm/that
  (1) By missives of sale and purchase dated .... and .... I agreed to sell and B [*design*] agreed to purchase the subjects known as ....
  (2) The said subjects of sale are not/are not part of/do not include a matrimonial home in relation to which a spouse of mine has occupancy rights.

Sworn/affirmed
by the above A at
.... on the .... day of   .... A
.... 19 .... before me
X [*design*] Notary Public.
.... X

3. Style of Affidavit in Connection with Security (Section 8(2), (2A))

I, A [*design*] make oath/do solemnly and sincerely affirm/that
  (1) By intimation in writing dated .... XY [*design*] offered to advance to me a loan of £ ...... to be secured over the subjects known as ....
  (2) [*Where the security was granted before December 30, 1985*] At the date of the said intimation and at the date hereof, no non-entitled spouse exists in respect of the said subjects.

or

(2) [*Where the security was granted on or after December 30, 1985*] The said subjects are not/are not part of/do not include a matrimonial home in relation to which a spouse of mine has occupancy rights.

Sworn/affirmed
by the above A at
.... on the .... day of .... A
.... 19 .... before me
X [*design*] Notary Public.
. X

4. Style of Renunciation of Occupancy Rights

I, A [*design*] spouse of B. [*design*] hereby renounce the occupancy rights to which I am or may become entitled in terms of the Matrimonial Homes (Family Protection) (Scotland) Act 1981 in the property known as ———being/intended to become a matrimonial home as defined in the said Act; And I hereby swear/affirm that this renunciation is made by me freely and without coercion of any kind; And I declare these presents to be irrevocable.

Signed by me at ———this ——— day of ——— 19—— in the presence of [*design*] Notary Public, and in the presence of these witnesses:—

. . . . Witness .... A
. . . . Full Name
. . . . Address
. . . . Occupation

. . . . Witness .... NP
. . . . Full Name
. . . . Address
. . . . Occupation

INDEX

[All references are to paragraph numbers]

Index

interim orders relating to, 2-46, 2-47
jurisdiction based on, 8-03
rights of non-entitled spouse in, 2-03 to
2-06, 2-22 to 2-25
sale of, 2-17, 2-65, 3-03, 6-05, 6-15, 6-16,
6-20, 6-22
security over, 6-05, 6-06, 6-18, 6-19
summary ejection from, 3-31
transfer of tenancy of, 4-02, 4-03

MATRIMONIAL INTERDICT,
breach of, 5-02, 5-10, 5-14, 5-15
definition of, 5-02
power of arrest attached to, 5-05 to 5-09
relationship with exclusion, 3-10 to 3-15,
5-03
service of, 5-07

NON-ENTITLED PARTNER (see COHABITING
PARTNER)
NON-ENTITLED SPOUSE,
alternative accommodation,
offer by entitled spouse, 2-33, 2-41, 3-18,
4-06, 6-10, 8-01
provision by local authority, 3-35 to 3-37
compensation,
payable to, for loss of rights, 2-48 to 2-51,
6-17, 8-04
payable by, on transfer of tenancy, 4-12
conduct of, 2-33, 2-41, 3-18, 4-06, 6-10,
8-01
consent in relation to calling-up, 8-02
consent to dealing by, 2-12, 2-17, 6-08,
6-22
definition of,
generally, 2-09 to 2-12, 2-17
in relation to dealings, 6-04
dispensing with consent of, 6-10 to 6-12,
6-16, 6-22
enforcement of obligation by, 2-22, 2-23
exclusion of (see EXCLUSION ORDER)
needs of, 2-33, 2-41, 3-18, 4-06, 6-10, 8-01
occupancy rights,
protection from dealings (see PROTECTION
FROM DEALINGS)
renunciation of, 2-59 to 2-63, 4-02, 6-09,
6-15, 6-16, 6-19, 6-22
payment by,
outgoings etc., 2-22
to heritable creditor, 2-22, 6-18
performance of obligations by, 2-22, 2-23
rights in relation to matrimonial home, 2-03,
2-22, 2-25
transfer of tenancy to, 4-02, 4-04
NOTICE OF DEFAULT, 7-10(h), 8-02

OBLIGATION,
enforcement of, 2-22, 2-23, 7-07
performance of, 2-22, 2-23, 7-07
OCCUPANCY RIGHTS,
cohabiting partner, 7-02 to 7-06
compensation for loss of, 2-48 to 2-51,
6-17, 7-08, 8-04
declarator of, 2-30
defending, by non-entitled spouse, 2-22

definition of, 2-03 to 2-06
enforcement of, 2-31 to 2-34
incident of marriage, 2-02
interim orders relating to, 2-46, 2-47
jointly entitled spouses, 2-64
note of absence in Land Register, 6-02, 6-17
protection of, 2-22, 2-37, 7-08 (see also
PROTECTION FROM DEALINGS)
regulation of, 2-36
renunciation of, 2-59 to 2-63, 4-02, 6-09,
6-15, 6-16, 6-19, 6-22
restriction of, 2-53
suspension of (see EXCLUSION ORDER)
termination of, 2-52 to 2-58, 6-17, 7-06,
7-10(b) to (d)
OUTGOINGS,
payment of, 2-22, 7-07
OVERRIDING INTEREST, 6-02

PARTNER (see COHABITING PARTNER)
POINDING, 2-43, 2-65, 7-10(f), 8-03
POLICE,
discretion to liberate, 5-15
power of arrest,
effect of, 5-10
notification of, 5-11 to 5-13
POWER OF ARREST,
attachment to interdict, 3-10, 5-01, 5-05,
5-06, 5-09, 7-07, 7-10(d)
effect of, 5-10
notification to police, 5-11 to 5-13
procedure following arrest, 5-14, 5-15
recall of, 5-07, 5-13
service of interdict, 5-07, 5-08
termination of, 5-07, 5-13

PRESCRIPTION OF OCCUPANCY RIGHTS, 2-55,
2-56, 6-17
PROCURATOR FISCAL, 5-14, 5-15
PROTECTION FROM DEALINGS,
ante-nuptial dealings, 6-13
cohabiting partner, 7-08
consent by spouse, 2-12, 2-17, 6-08, 6-22
consent dispensed with, 6-10 to 6-12, 6-16,
6-22
definition of dealing, 6-05, 6-06
general scope of, 6-01 to 6-03
post-divorce, 2-65
pre-Act dealing, 6-14
renunciation by spouse, 2-63, 6-09
sale of matrimonial home, 6-15, 6-16, 6-22
security over matrimonial home, 6-06,
6-18, 6-19
tenanted home, 6-03, 6-05, 6-06

REGISTER OF SASINES, 6-01, 6-02, 6-22
REGULATION OF OCCUPANCY RIGHTS, 2-36,
7-07
RENT,
apportionment of, 2-26 to 2-28, 2-64,
7-10(b)
arrears of on transfer of tenancy, 4-05,
4-07, 4-08, 4-13
payment of, 2-22, 7-07
RENT (SCOTLAND) ACT 1984, 2-08, 2-44

[93]